Wood Burning
for
Beginners

Table of Contents

Introduction

Pyrography or wood burning is an ancient art that has been widely adopted globally. Pyrography is a unique skill for decorating wood by applying enough heat to wood so that burn marks are created according to the detail in your design. Pyrographers control the way heat is applied to wood to create the desired shades and tones. Pyrography is a common term used to describe wood burning on a wide range of surfaces, and wood burning exclusively refers to wood.

Wood burning art forms have been as ancient as cavemen. It is believed that cavemen created drawings with charred sticks. Pyrography was recognized as an art hundreds of years ago. During those days, craftsmen placed metal pokers in hot coals of fire. They would wait for the pokers to get red hot and start burning wood when the poker reached a temperature ideal for burning wood. The art of pyrography gained popularity during the 17th century. Ever since, artists have used many different techniques to create burn marks on wood such as focusing sunlight on a magnifying lens to generate heat for wood burning, using a metal tool heated by fire, or using specialized tools designed for the purpose. Pyrography received true recognition in the Victorian era.

Pyrography allows a high-level of creativity. To become a successful pyrographer, it is important to understand different techniques used in shading and shadows, and be able to successfully create different forms of artwork, ranging from simple signboards to detailed landscapes and portraits.

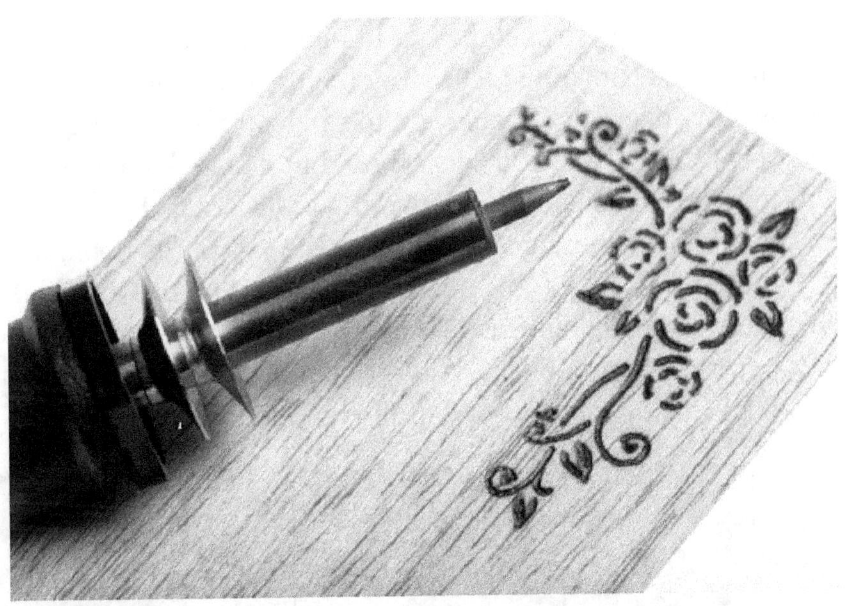

This book teaches you important skills to master the art of pyrography. It takes you through a step-by-process to acquire basic skills in a wide range of pyrography art forms. Tips and tricks are available for artists and crafters and serve as starting points for designing professional masterpieces.

The goal of this book is to enable you with the required resources and information to be able to design pyrography projects. The whole process is described in a step-by-step manner, supported by relevant illustrations. You will learn everything from choosing the right materials and tools, to following proven techniques that help achieve the desired shade and texture on wood.

"Wood burning for Beginners" covers basic burn tools and types of wood available, and demonstrates the correct use of tools including safety precautions. It teaches you how to make your own pyro-pen with a basic USB cable and syringe needles. Basic line art and shading techniques are covered to help you understand the essence of the artwork.

Further, the use of stencils and image transfer techniques are discussed. Burning Lichtenberg figures as a modern artform is also covered to enable you to safely implement the technique. Other projects covered in the book include burning a basic mandala, making a Christmas Box, and making fridge magnets. Towards the end of the book, more techniques to shading and line art are explained and ideas to burn common landscape are covered. Finally, pursuing pyrography as a business is discussed and ways to promote your business online and offline is explained in detail.

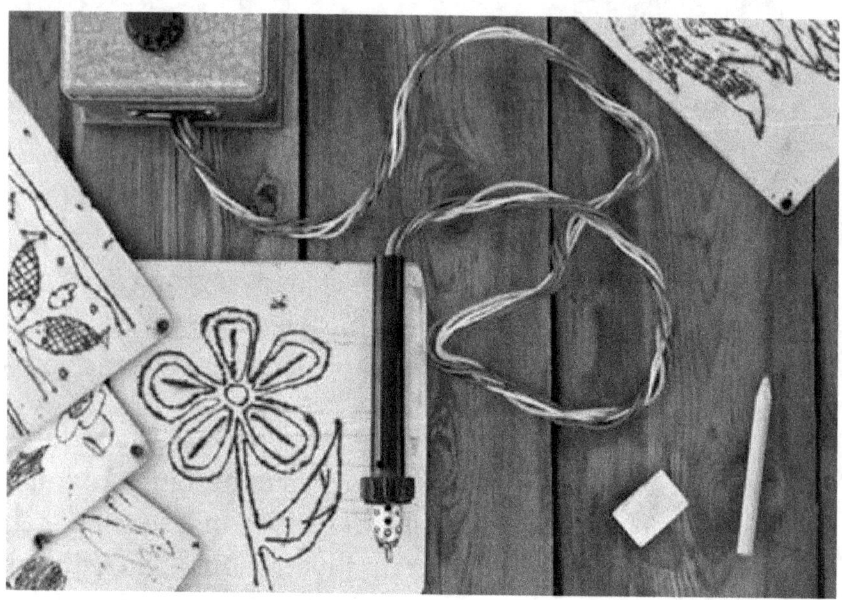

Chapter One:
History of Pyrography

Pyrography, or the technique of wood burning traces its linguistic origin to the Greek language. It is derived from the words "pur", which means fire, and "graphos",which means writing.

Pyrography, also known as pyrogravur, is a traditional art of burning wood surfaces using heated metal tools. The art may be simply referred to as wood burning, or sometimes, pokerwork and is chiefly used as a decorative art for wooden items such as utensils and furniture.

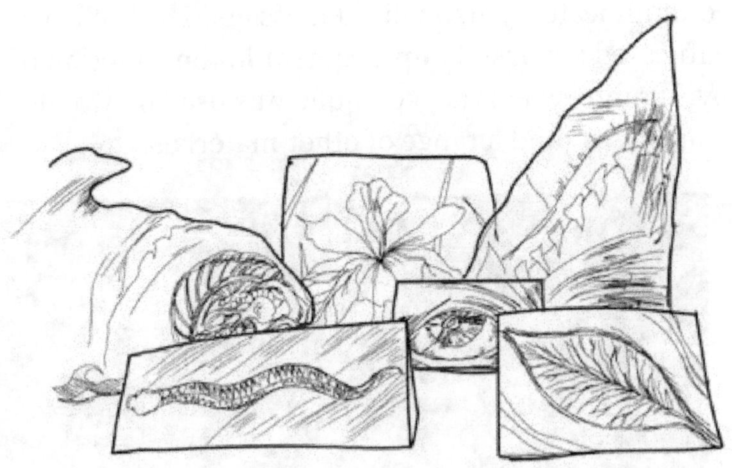

History of Pyrography

The art of wood burning has been around for many years. The term was first coined in the 1900s. Pyrography has been an essential part of cultures around the world, in the regions of China, Rome, Peru, and Egypt.

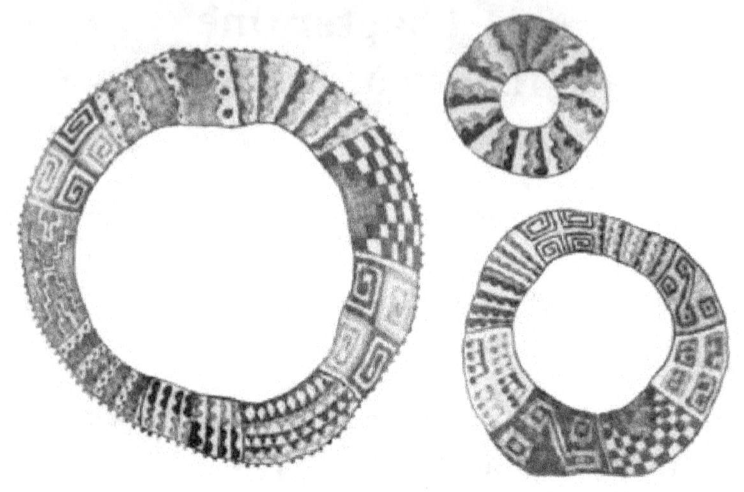

The purpose of pyrography was originally to decorate musical instruments and tools to impart an artistic look and communicate a personalized message. The Victorian era witnessed a marked improvement in the adoption of pyrography when the technique was used on wood "canvasses" and a range of other materials.

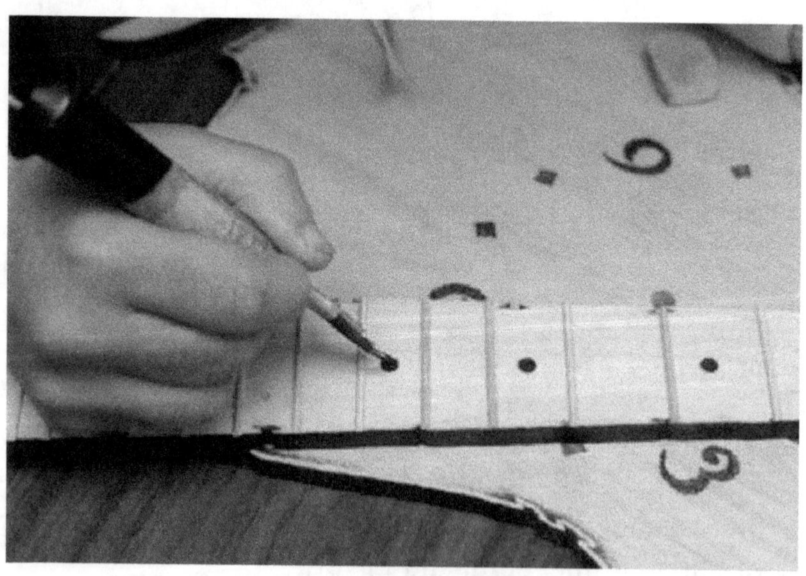

Pyrography was essentially a male-dominated art until the late 19th century. It was during this time that pyrography kits and machines were used in homes, marking a significant involvement of women in the art of wood burning. Women mostly used the pyrography technique to decorate their houses with beautiful hand-crafted artwork.

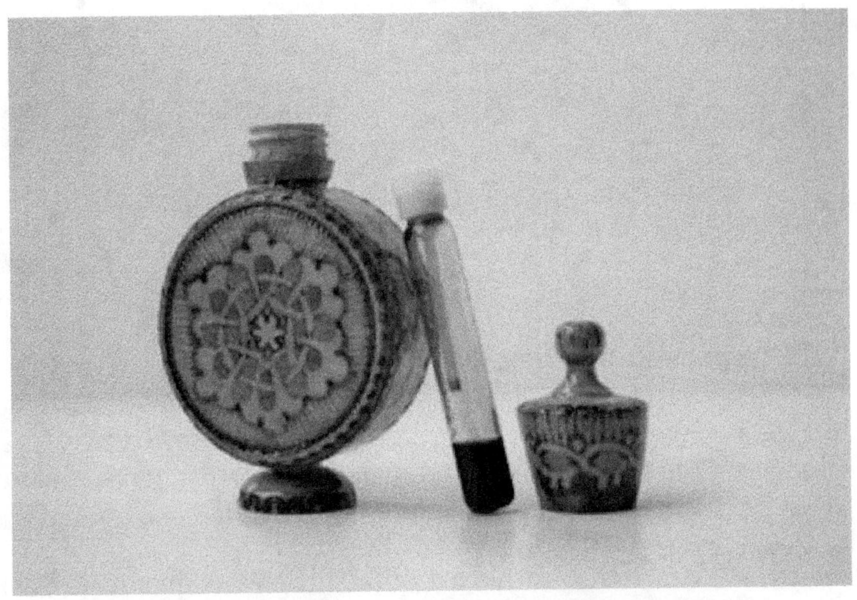

During this time, the art was popularized through magazines and printed publications to encourage young artists to embrace the technique. Pyrography kits were also sold at reasonable prices to provide the means to decorate homes or sell hand-crafted items. Women engaged in different types of projects, from handkerchief boxes and picture frames, to chairs and cabinets. Thereafter, pyrography became an integral part of fine craftsmanship across cultures and continents globally.

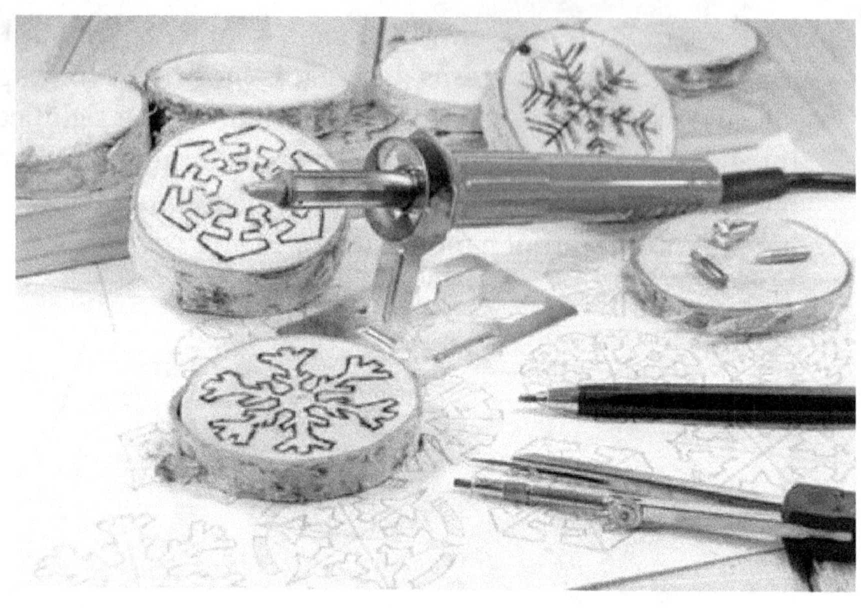

Chapter Summary

- Pyrography is a word derived from the Greek language. It is composed of the words "pur", meaning fire and "graphos" meaning writing.

- It is a traditional art of burning wooden surfaces with heated metal tools

- Initially, artisans decorated musical instruments with pyrography artwork to put across personalized messages

- Pyrography was widely adopted globally during the 19th century as magazines and publications served as tools to promote the ancient technique

In the next chapter you will learn about basic tools and techniques used in pyrography: selecting an appropriate wood base to burn your pyrography artwork, selecting the right burn tool, and the burn tip.

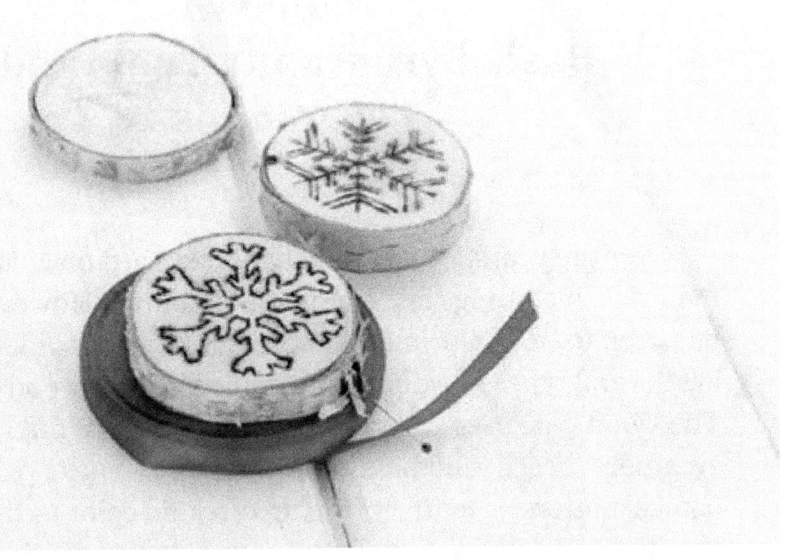

Chapter Two:
Basic Pyrography Tools and Techniques

Over the years, pyrography has been used on a variety of materials including clay, leather, and gourds. However, wood has been used as a primary medium for pyrography. There are several types of wood that may be used for wood burning. The wood type used in pyrography ranges from birch, sycamore, beech, and basswood, to pine and oak. Wood choice matters as it affects the texture and color of the final product.

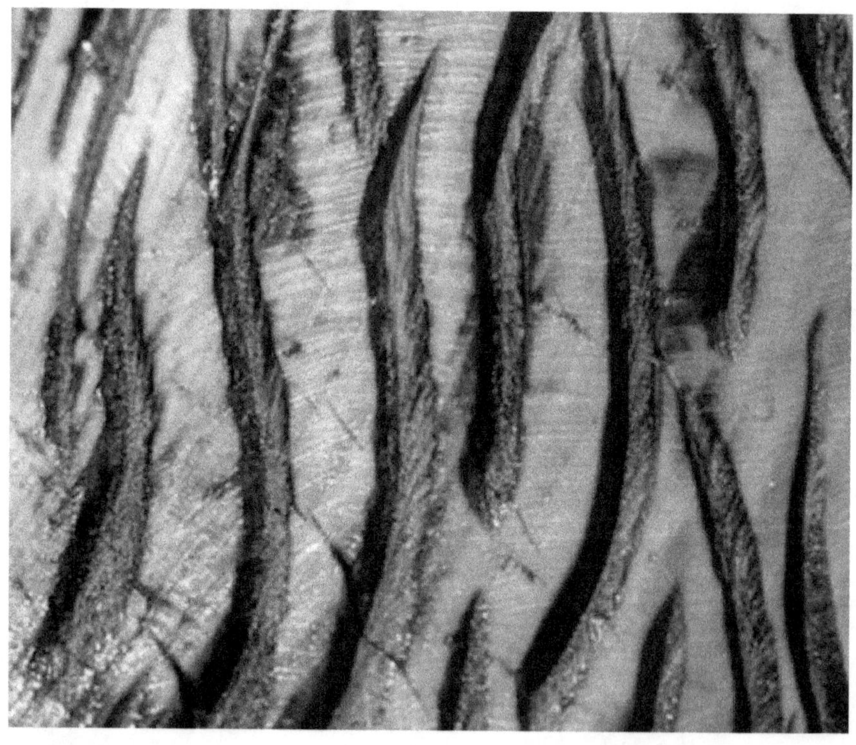

Professionals have different opinions on the options available, as the process produces different textures and colors based on the type of wood used. If you are looking for a particular look and feel for your artwork, then it is important to first understand the different types of wood available for the purpose.

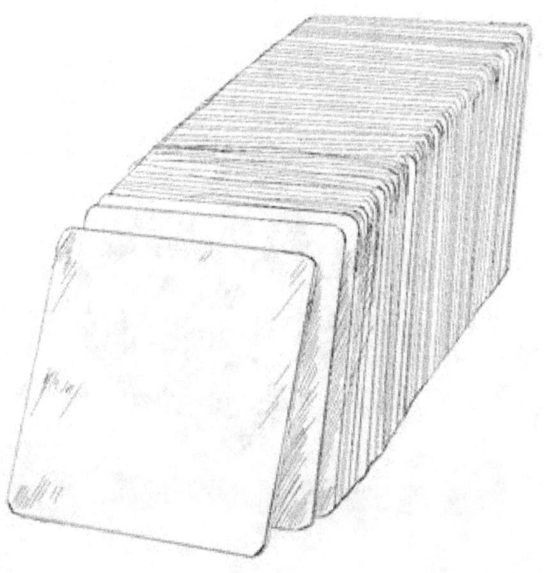

Baswood: Baswood is essentially softwood and does not contain a lot of grain. It is light-colored and has a clean appearance. These characteristics make baswood easy to burn. When working with baswood, you are likely to achieve an appearance very close to what you imagined when you started out. You can successfully burn light and dark portions with a high level of precision. Baswood is usually available online in different sizes such as plaques or circular pieces.

Maple: If you are ready to invest a significant amount of money for your artwork, then maple wood may work for you. Maple has important features that tend to enhance your artwork. It's light to medium color and subtle grain achieve a good finish even with intricate burning. However, you must consider the fact that the wood has a significant level of hardness, and may require very high temperatures to get the desired results.

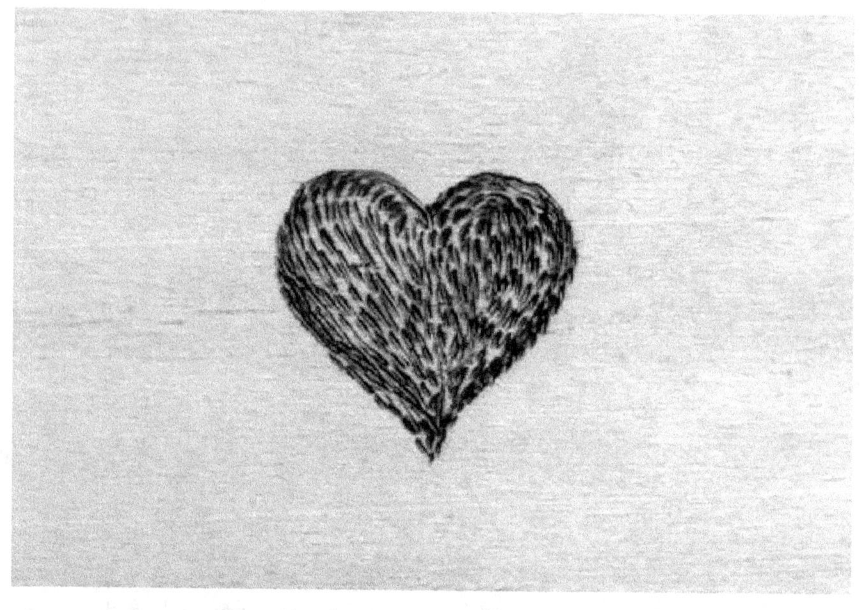

Poplar: Poplar is preferred by most pyrographers as it is less costly when compared to maple. It burns quickly and is available in the desired quantity and size with little effort. It has soft and consistent grain, making it easy to achieve fine details. It is also possible to stain the wood with a high level of perfection. However, poplar may occasionally betray the artist when spots of sap or resin show up, or due to color streaking. Nevertheless, most artists tend to manage quite well with poplar and it's concerns are only regarded as a minor issue.

Beech: Beech is another good choice and may serve as a good replacement for poplar or maple. It has a pale color and a prominent grain pattern. Beech also contains sap as a constituent and heat may cause sap leaks, making it difficult to work with.

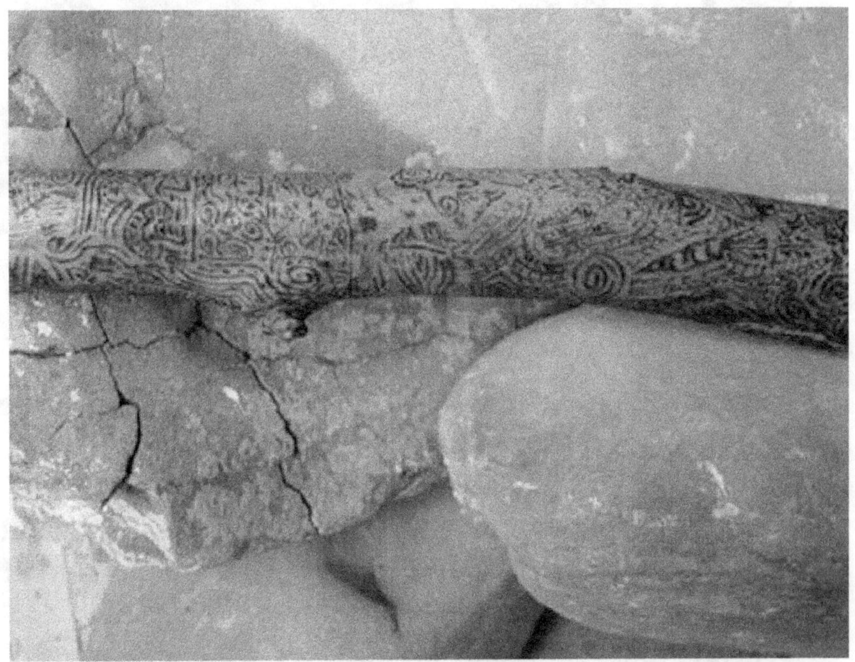

Birch: Birch is another option that is similar to baswood and contains soft grain that gives it a consistent look. Birch may not provide a high contrast as it is darker than other woods. Birch also requires higher burning temperatures when compared to baswood and poplar. It comes in different qualities, grades, and tones.

Red Oak: Red Oak has a different texture, in that it is tough and may be a challenge for the pyrographer. The wood also contains more moisture than other types of wood. Sap leaks from its surface may sometimes make the woodwork look messy.

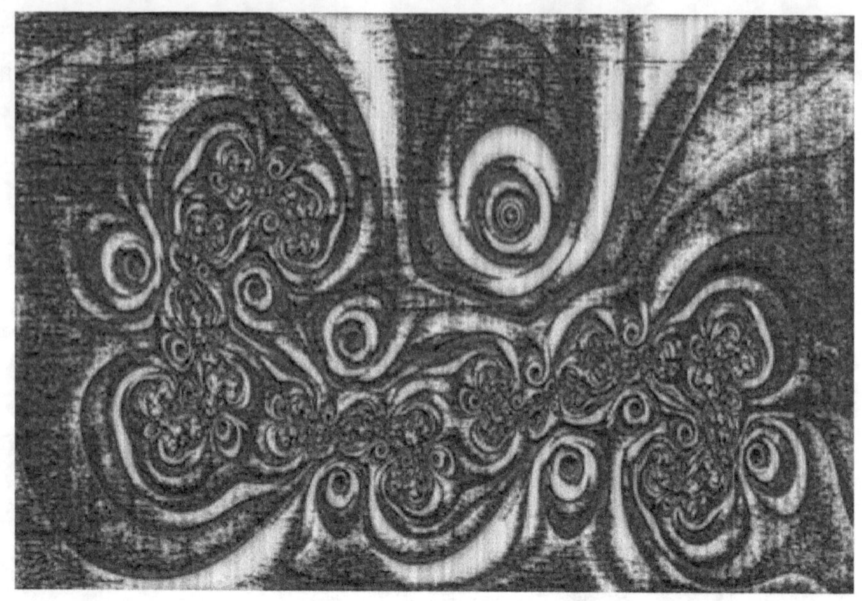

Pine: Pine is an inexpensive option for pyrographers and is available in a wide variety of sizes, shapes, and designs. Pine comes with different types of grain. While pine with darker grain may be difficult to burn, a lighter grain is often characteristic to soft wood. Pine is generally preferable when burning solid letters or signboards. It is important to consider that yellow pine produces a low-quality finished product. Furthermore, white pine is softwood and produces a smooth burn.

To sum it all up, grainy or dark woods are less forgiving for the pyrographer. Woods that contain resins may also pose problems on heating their surface. Further, woods that have been chemically treated or contain synthetic materials tend to emit toxic chemicals when heated. Therefore, it is best to avoid pre-treated wood.

Choosing the Right Wood Burner

Several types of wood burning tools have been in use across the ages. Heated metal rods were the tools used initially to burn the desired design on wood. During the middle ages, the primary heat source used by most artists was a wooden stove. Pokers were placed through small holes in the lids of the stove. Pokers were heated by the heat from coal placed under the stove to achieve the desired artwork. Artists also used needles and knives besides pokers to burn the wood. Pyrography and blacksmithing were closely related during these times. The latter was often used to craft metal as well as wood.

It was during the 20th century that Alfred Smart, an architect based in Melbourne introduced the use of benzene fumes pumped through a heated, hollow pencil, allowing it to retain heat throughout the wood burning process. Pyrography pencils were made from platinum and connected to a benzene bottle and rubber ball to push fumes through the pencil. This technique helped the art of pyrography to reach a new level as artists were able to use different tints and shades when burning wood.

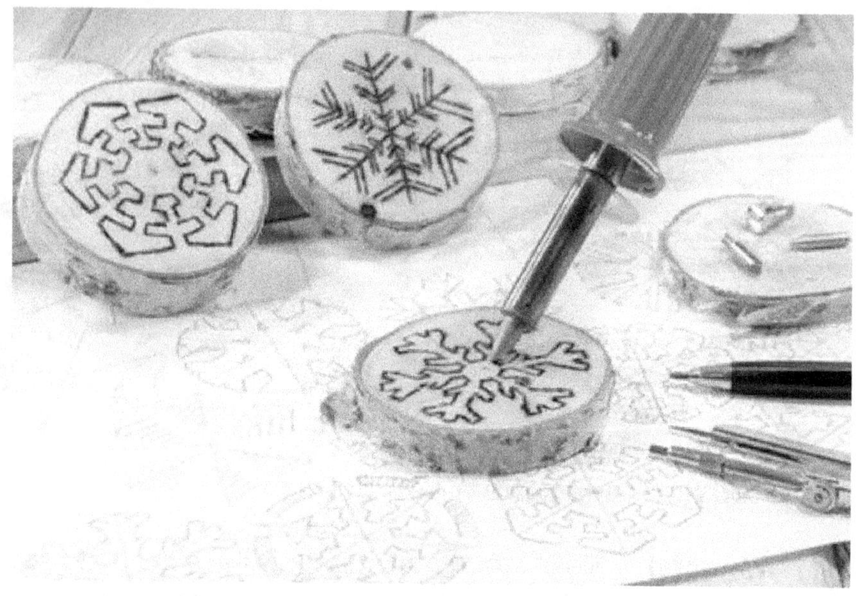

Over the years, wood burning tools have been enhanced to achieve the desired aesthetic effect on wood. Contemporary wood burners may be classified as wire nib burners, solid point burners, and laser cutters.

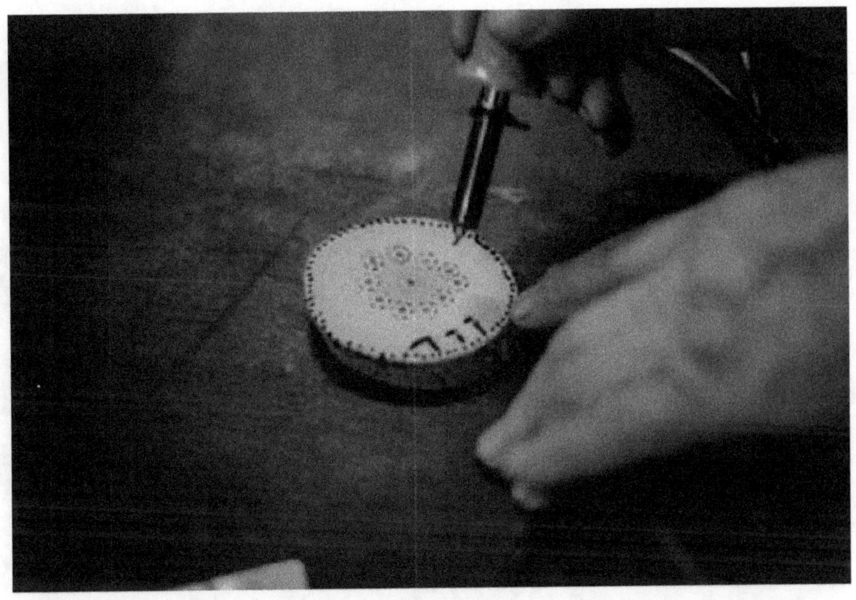

Solid Point Wood Burners : A solid-point wood-burning pen is an affordable and popular wood burning tool. The solid-point wood burning pen is very similar to a soldering iron, and consists of a definite soldering tip. The pen contains all the heating components in its body and is bulky. A solid-point burner features either a screw-in-tip or a non-screw-in-tip secured using a nut and sleeve.

Tips for solid-point wood-burning pens feature different threads types identified by specific configurations. A solid-point pen with M4 X0.7 tips refers to a pen with a thread measuring 4mm in diameter and a thread pitch measuring 0.7mm. Tips may have to be secured using pliers to be effective.

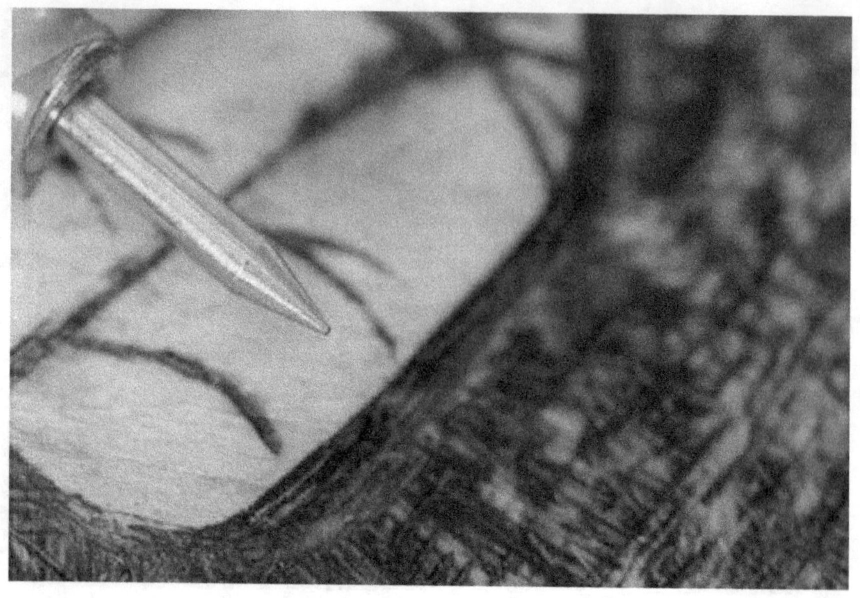

Solid-point burners are quite affordable and come with multiple patterns for their tips. They are usually manufactured with brass tips, which are good conductors of heat. Tips can be screwed and unscrewed and the solid-point pens produce a variable heat output. Solid-point pens also have less risk of shortening.

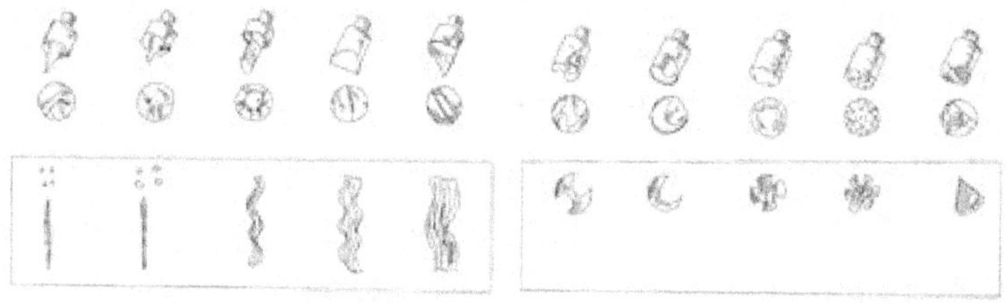

Further, solid-point pens are convenient to work with as they contain a non-slip rubber grip. The pens feature protection from heat for the hands. Double heat sinks and ventilation holes together provide the required protection against overheating. When working with solid-point pens, you must ensure you put just enough pressure to prevent the heated brass tip from softening, bending, or breaking. It is always essential to understand how heat can achieve the right shading and tone as opposed to pressing down the brass tip to achieve the artistic effect. This strategy also ensures that the brass tip does not break due to excessive pressure.

Another important consideration before investing in a solid-point pen is that it features only two power settings, 15 watts and 30 watts. This means that the pen may take several minutes (as many as 3-4 minutes) to either heat up or cool down. Finally some artists may not find the pen convenient to work with as their hands are farther away from the work surface when compared to wire-nib burners.

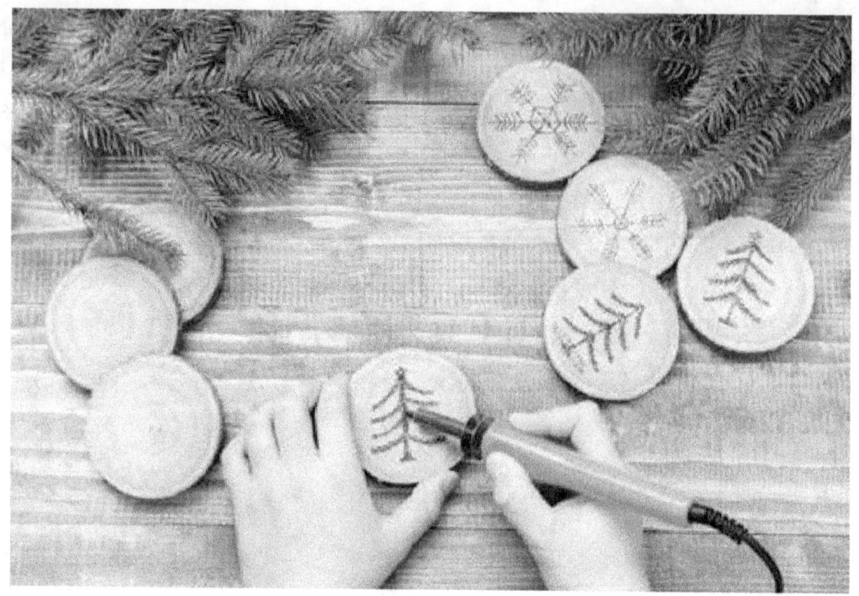

Wire-Nib Burners: A wire-nib burner consists of wire tips made from Ni-chrome wire with a specific gauge. Wires are usually secured with screws. Heat is produced due to the electric current that goes through the wire nibs. Heating in wire-nib burners takes less time when compared to solid-point tip pens. Consequently, they take less time to cool down, and it is quite simple and easy to remove and insert wire nibs. They work well even in high voltage settings, and artists get the freedom to practice with a variety of nib sizes and shapes. Wire-nib burners also allow artists to use customized nibs using Ni-chrome wire.

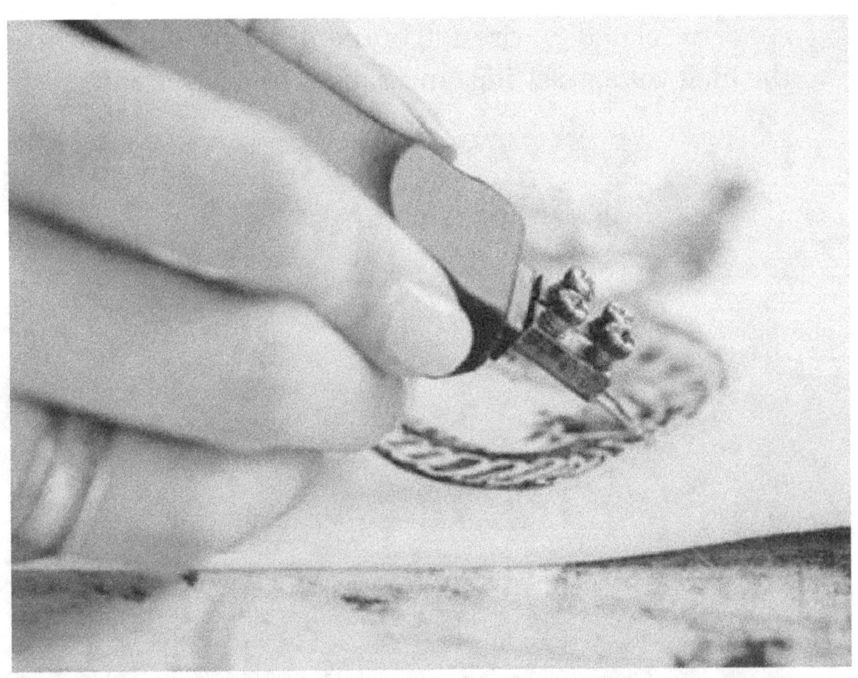

Wire-nib pens allow the artist to stay very close to the work surface. The pens rely on a digital-power supply that can be calibrated precisely for optimal heat output for the tip. This mechanism also allows the artist to have greater control over the burn. Wire-nib burners are also lighter and smaller than solid-point burners. Nib sizes suitable for wire-nib burners are 20GA measuring 0.8mm in diameter, and 16GA measuring 1.25mm in diameter. The Ni-chrome wire nibs do not tend to break easily on applying pressure and they come with non-slip rubber handles for an effective grip.

On the downside, wire-nib burners cost more than solid-point pens, and do not have ready-to-use patterns. Furthermore, wire-nib burners have a bulky power supply. Beginners may find them challenging when they are not able to use heat on the nib fast enough, as the burners may become uncomfortable to handle. Moreover, another major concern related to wire-nib burners is their danger in using the high voltage setting, and danger from shortening.

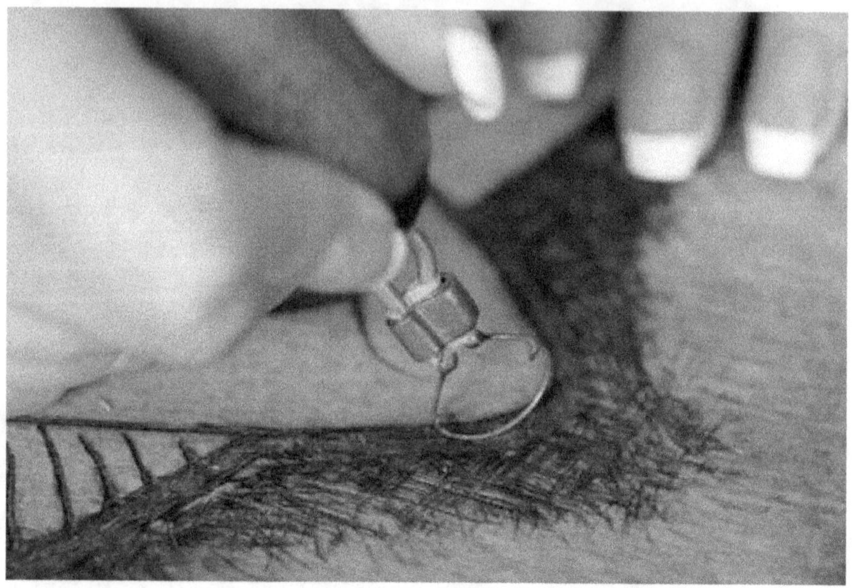

Laser Wood Burning Pen: A laser wood burning pen consists of a mechanical pencil with a high-power laser diode. Laser wood burning machines generally cost more than other wood burners. You can achieve a precise and exact representation of what you imagined with a laser wood burner. To effectively use the laser wood burner or engraver, you may either create the desired design using a software that provides the computer aided design (CAD) capability, or rely on the software provided with the equipment. When choosing a software, it is important to consider which one costs less, allows more creativity, and supports the required fonts and designs.

Furthermore, since laser wood burners come with a wide range of features, it is important to consider which machine will be most suitable for your choice of wood and project. Other considerations before purchasing the right wood burner include its size or space requirements and the way in which it interfaces with your computer system, specifically using either a wireless interface such as Bluetooth, a wired connection, or a USB connection.

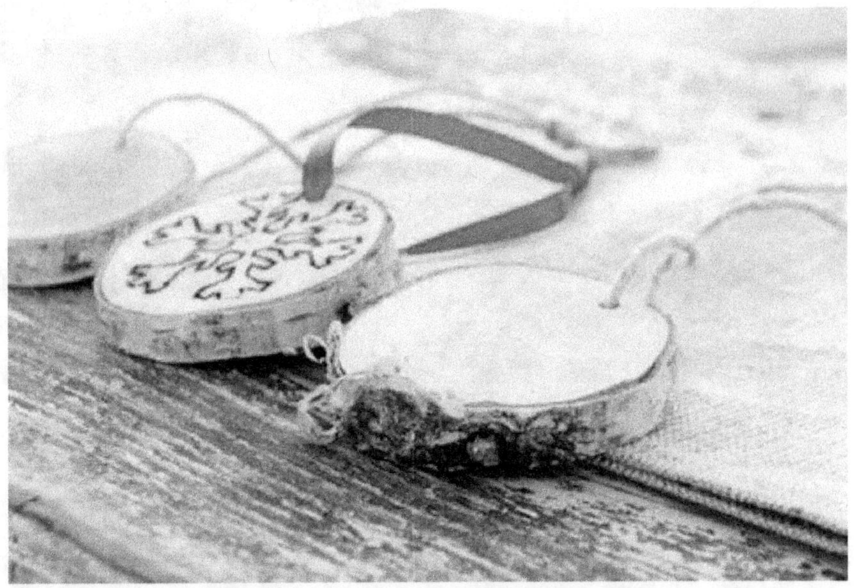

Wrapping it all up, solid-point burners often prove useful for novice artists. As you gain experience in the art after investing a significant number of hours practicing the art, it's best to invest in a wire-nib burner considering its pros and cons discussed above. Laser wood burning pens serve useful at a stage when you have understood the basic characteristics of wood and the process of wood burning, so as to incorporate automation in the skill.

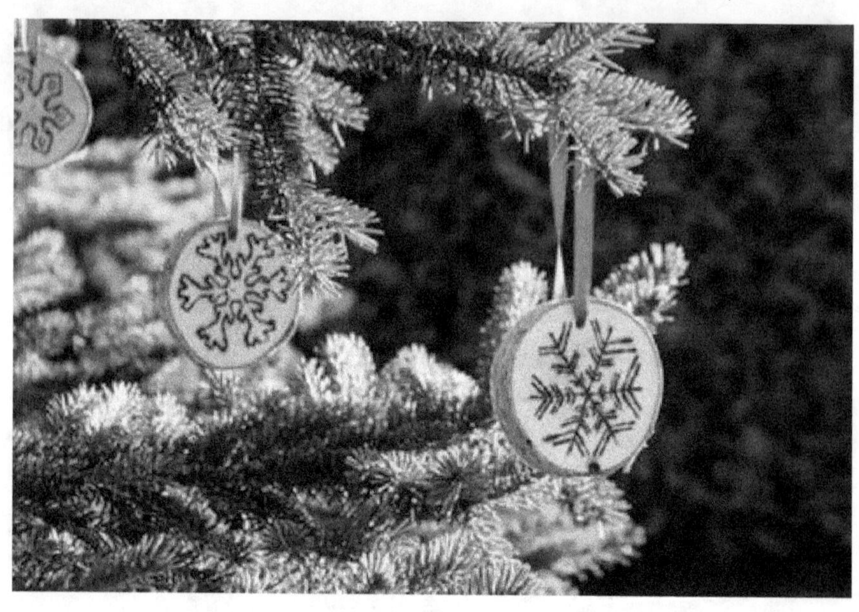

Safety Tips for Wood Burning

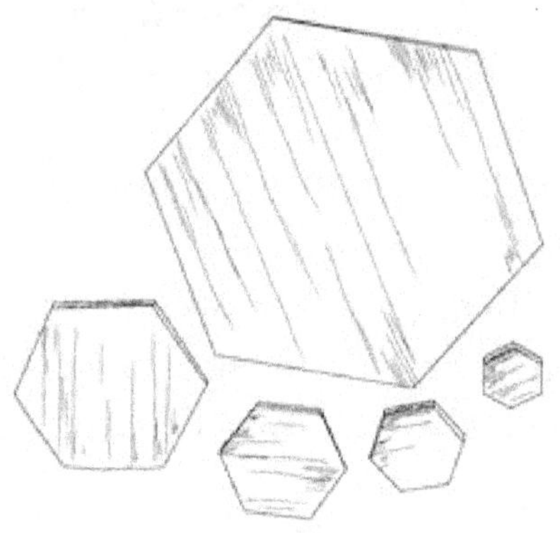

It is extremely essential to exercise certain precautions when burning wood.

First, invest in a good facemask that contains filters. Face masks protect against smoke and fumes that may emanate while burning wood.

Further, the area used for wood burning must be well-ventilated. Big windows that open wide and let fresh air in provide the best ventilation. An exhaust fan may be installed in one of the windows to suck out smoke and keep the working area smelling fresh and clean. Good air flow is the best way to avoid toxic smoke or fumes.

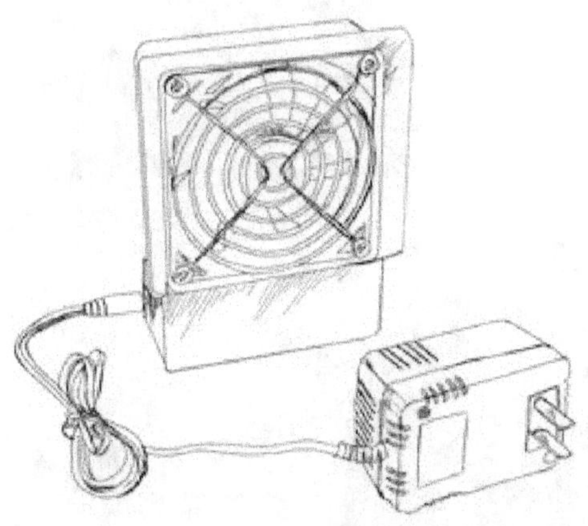

Another important safety tip in pyrography is to use a fan as it protects against breathing smoke for hours while working with wood. The fan need not be expensive, and even a small battery-operated fan serves the purpose well. The fan essentially keeps the smoke away from the face and protects you from developing irritable eyes or any sort of breathing problems.

That said, you may exercise caution when working with pallet wood. As you move forward with the art of pyrography, you are likely to encounter pallet wood. Pallet wood is essentially wood that has come in contact with chemicals, either by way of chemical treatment, while carrying chemicals during transport, or in cases when chemicals may have leaked on its surface. When the wood comes in contact with any type of chemicals, it may give rise to important concerns. In effect, neither burning the wood nor breathing the smoke and fumes as it burns, may be safe. To work with pallet wood, a good quality face mask that contains filters is a mandatory safety requirement. Further, as discussed above, the area must be well-ventilated, and it is preferable to use a fan to avoid breathing toxic fumes.

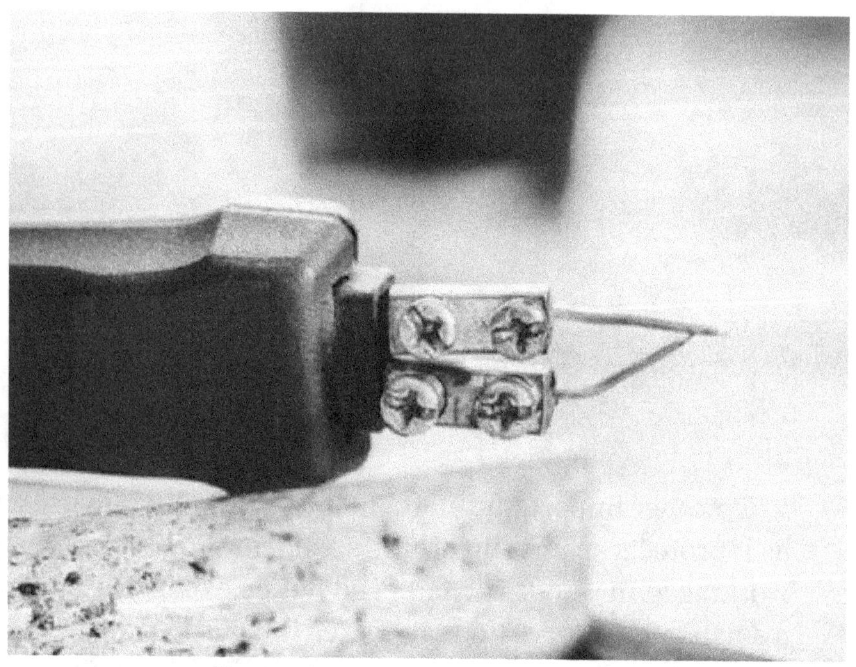

Chapter Summary

- Wood has different characteristics. Selecting the right wood for your pyrography projects depends on a close scrutiny of its features.

    - Baswood is less grainy and light-colored. It burns easily with a high level of precision.

    - Maple has a medium shade with subtle grain. It is hard wood and requires higher burning temperatures, although intricate designs are still possible on maple wood.

- o Poplar is an economical option for pyrography. It is soft with consistent grain and burns easily. It is ideal for staining and precision wood burning. Sap from wood may sometimes interfere with the wood burning.

  - o Beech has a pale color and prominent grain pattern, but may create issues from sap leaks.

  - o Birch has soft grain, provides high contrast, and burns with higher temperatures. It differs in terms of tone, quality and grade.

  - o Red oak contains more moisture, and artists may find it challenging to deal with its sap leaks.

  - o Pine comes with dark as well as light grain. Pine quality varies considerably.

- Pyrographers generally work with three different burners:

  - o Solid point wood burners are popular and affordable. All heating components are encapsulated in its pen. They come with different patterns for their pen tips. Consider the different power settings supported by solid point woodburners (15 watts and 30 watts) before investing.

  - o Wire-nib burners are made from NiChrome wire. They come in a variety of shapes and sizes, and can withstand high voltage. They carry the danger of shortening.

  - o Laser wood burning pens consist of mechanical pencils with a high-power laser diode. They are precise, and most suitable for precision and intricate pyrography.

- Safety is a priority in wood burning. Remember essential precautions for a rewarding experience:

  o Invest in face masks with filters.

  o Work in a well-ventilated area.

  o Use a fan to keep smoke away from your face and avoid inhaling it.

  o Install an exhaust to ensure that your work area and clean and free from smoke

  o Pre-treated wood (pallet wood) is known to cause problems during burning by emitted toxic smoke. A face mask is highly recommended while working with pallet wood.

In the next chapter you will learn about the different types of wood burners, how to use the different burn tips, how to hold your wood burning pen, and change burn tips.

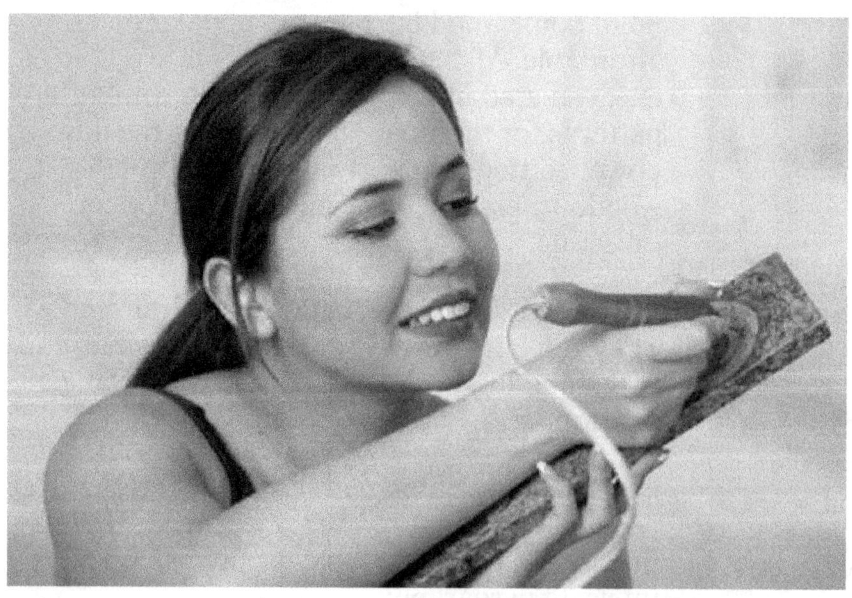

Chapter Three:
How to Use a Wood Burner

The most important aspect of pyrography is to know how to effectively use your wood burner to get the desired look and feel of your artwork. To understand how wood burners work, it is essential to explore the different tips used in wood burners and also learn how to hold a wood burning tool. Finally, you can achieve professional pyrography artwork by understanding how to change wood burner tips.

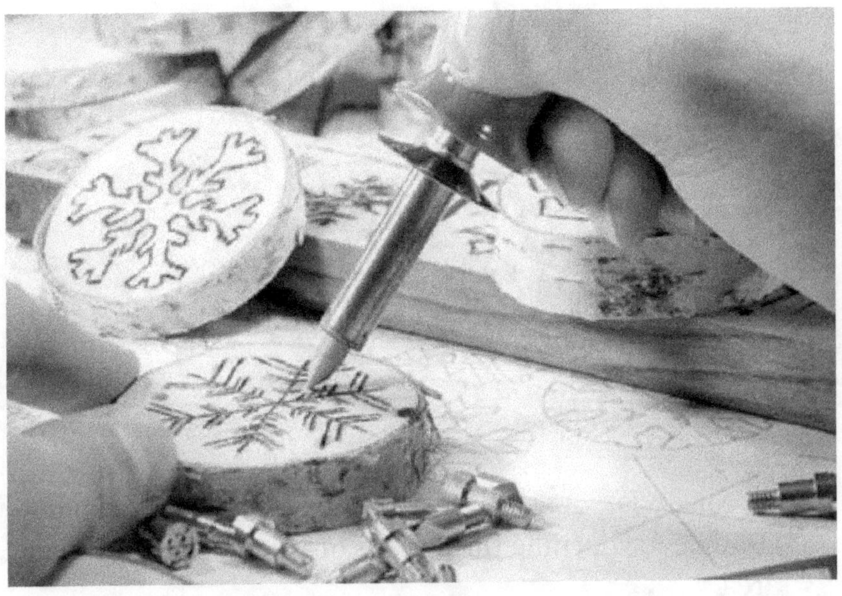

Overview of Burning Tips in Different Types of Wood Burners

Several types of wood burning tips are available to create the best pyrography artwork. Wood burning tips are measured in terms of wire gauges, and a thicker wire is identified by a smaller gauge. Thicker wires take more time to heat up when compared to thinner wires. This means that a wire tip measuring 20-gauge heats up faster than the one measuring 16-gauge. The choice of basic tip styles and shapes for wood burning depends on the type of wood burner used.

Tips used for wire-nib burners may be one of the five types described below.

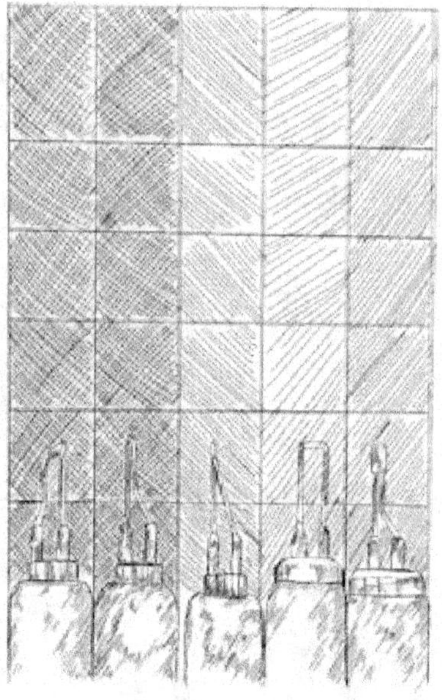

Spear Tip: A spear tip features a pointed edge and is suitable for burning fine details or when designing a small area.

Skew Tip: A skew tip is a slanted tip with an angle. The tip is useful when defining long lines such as the feathers of a bird.

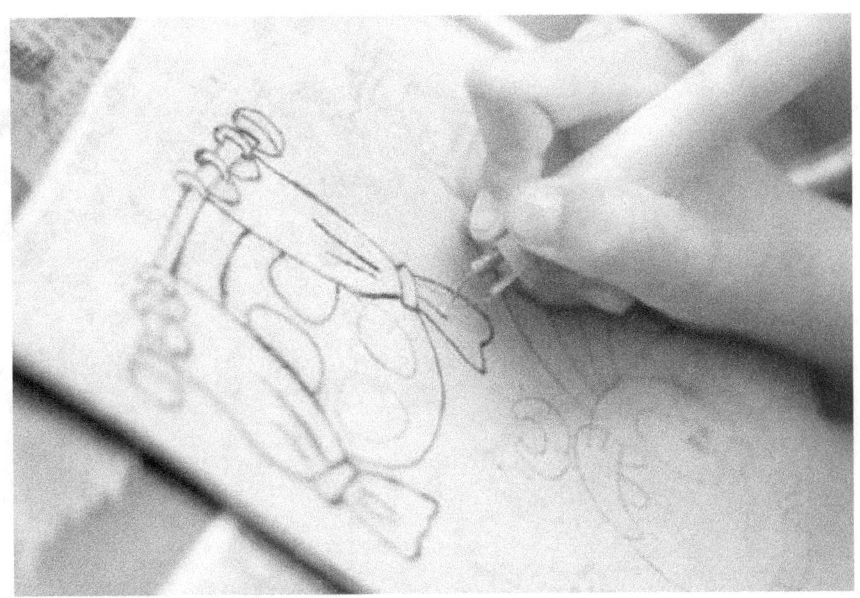

Round Tip: A round tip features a circular point and is useful when you do not need a depression in the detail you are trying to burn.

Chisel Tip: Chisel tips have burning edges that are at an angle perpendicular to the tool. One example of using the chisel tip is when working with quill lines.

Ballpoint Tip: The ballpoint tip features a small ball attached to the end of the tip. The tip is useful when working on designs that require a natural writing motion.

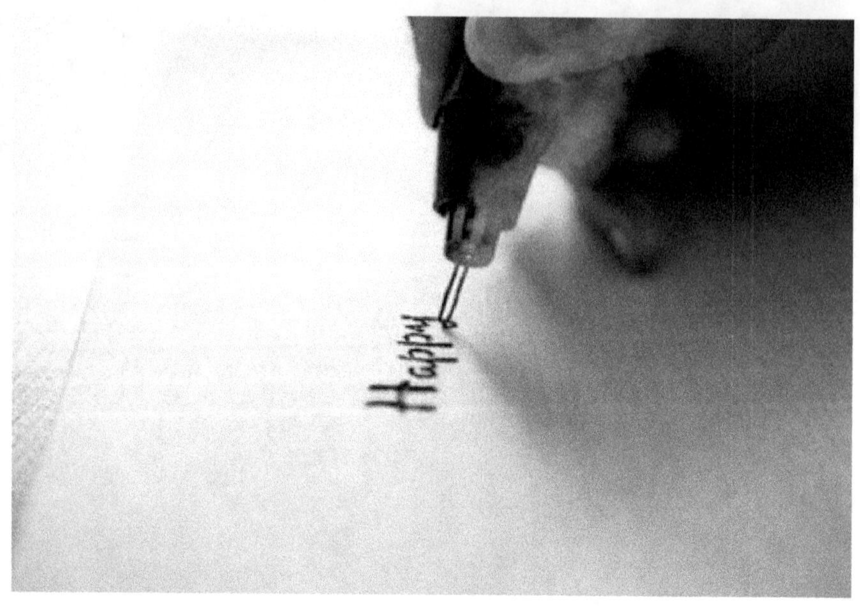

On the other hand, one of the following four tips may be used with solid-point burners.

Universal Tip: A universal tip serves as an all-purpose tip and is most suitable for burning outlines or straight lines for pyrography projects.

Extra-Fine Tip: When working with fine details of your artwork, the extra-fine tip serves as an indispensable tool to create definite curves and lines.

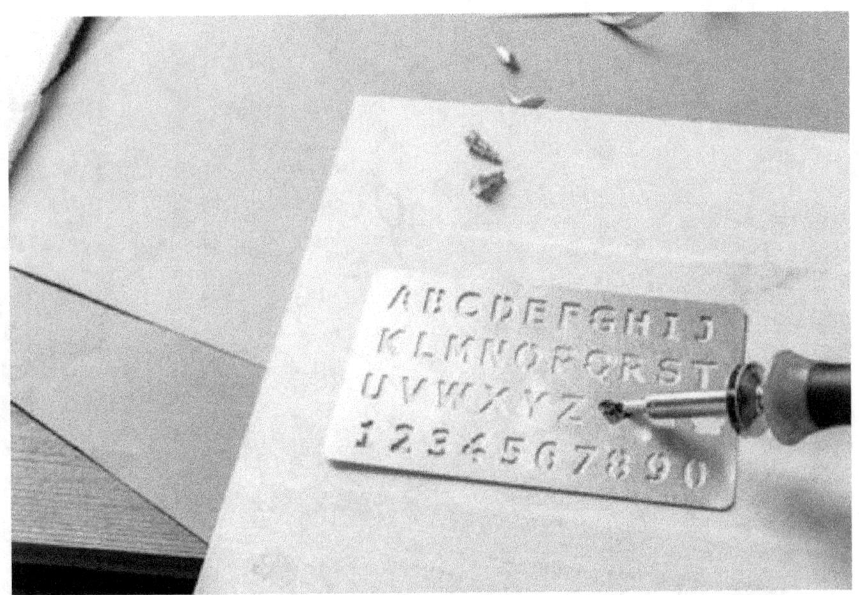

Shading Tip: A shading tip may be useful when creating a shading effect to cover large areas of your artwork. The shading tip is also effective when working with shadows.

Calligraphy Tip: The calligraphy tip is most suitable for drawing curved lines or when working with signboards and incorporating natural writing into your artwork.

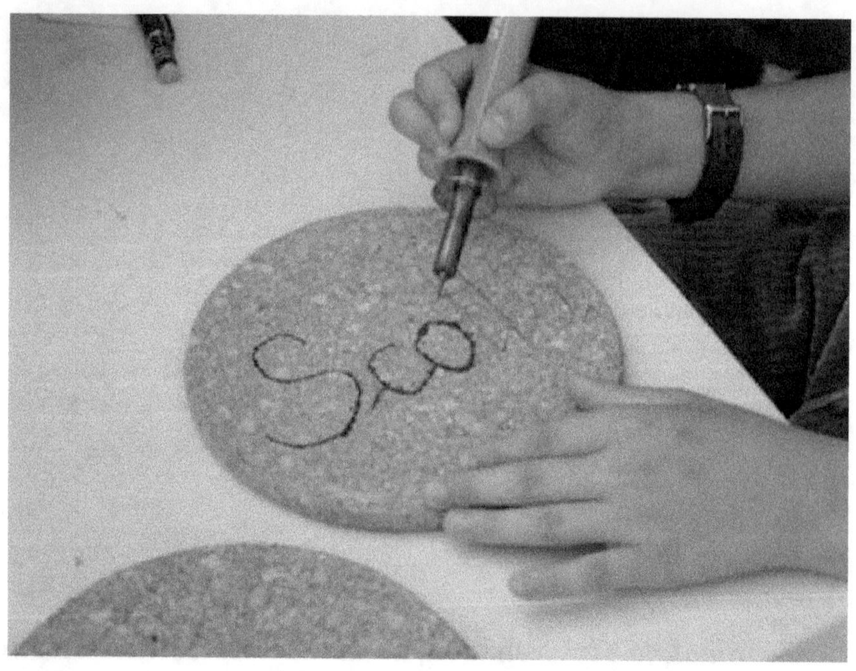

When working with the different types of tips for wood burners, the wood type you are working with determines how fast or slow it will burn. If you are using soft wood that has a low density (such as baswood), you will realise that it burns much faster. This feature implies that woods with low density and a high degree of softness require a small amount of heat to be applied. As wood gets denser and harder, such as in the case of oak or maple, you will need to apply more heat to achieve the same result. The burn process is also slower for hard woods. Further, woods that have low grain help you achieve a better contrast.

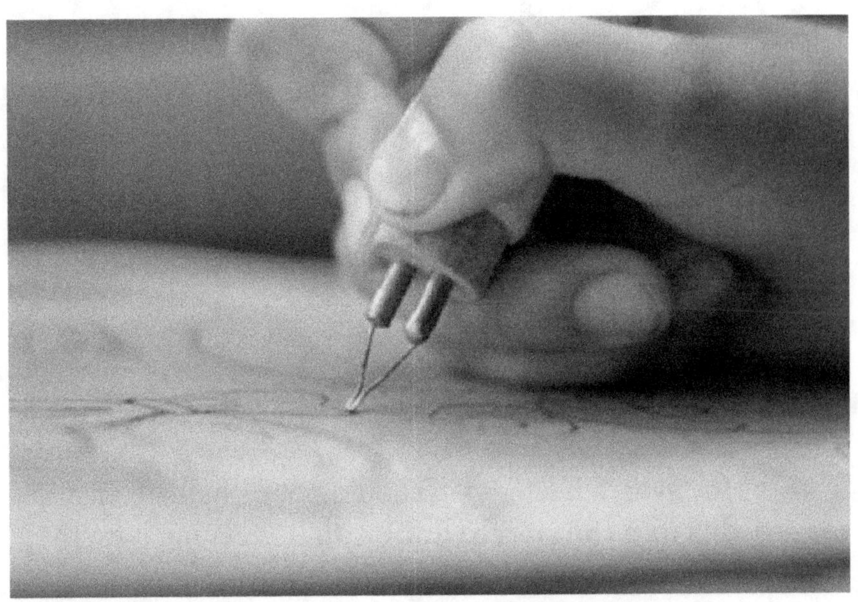

How to Hold and Use a Wood Burning Tool Effectively

The process of wood burning starts with sanding the desired piece of wood to achieve the desired smoothness. Thereafter, you may transfer your design on the wood using a soft pencil, graphite paper, or carbon paper.

Once you have your design on wood, the right technique must be used to hold your pen against the piece of wood. A wood burning pen is held much like a pen.

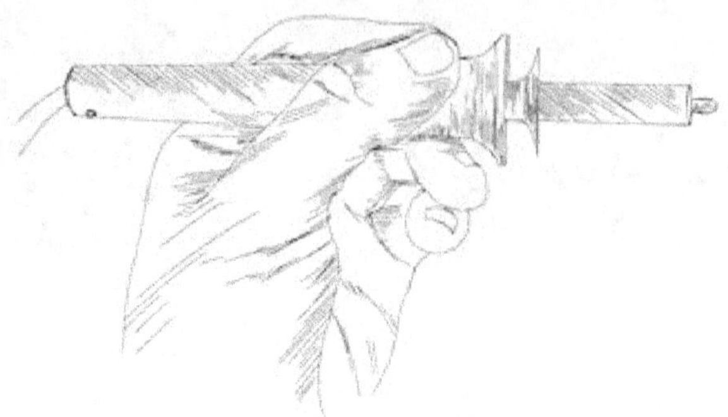

However, a heated pen should not be held against the wood before you start to draw with it. Keeping it on the surface even for a couple of seconds creates a blob. Therefore, the pen is most effective when using it with a "landing – take off" motion.

Before starting the wood burning process, attach the desired pen tip with pliers and heat the pen. Start burning the outline and fill spaces either by shading them or just filling them in a single tone. An important consideration when achieving the shading effect is to darken the required area using a gradual, circular motion using medium heat.

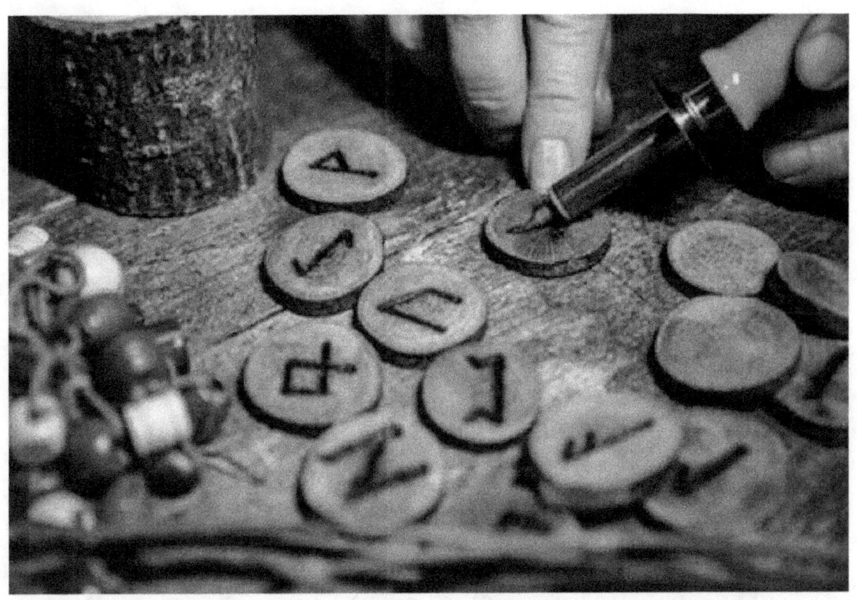

In general, woods that have grain tend to offer some resistance whenever you encounter the grain. When trying to work with wood that has grain, you may be able to achieve the best results by working with the grain, as opposed to working against it.

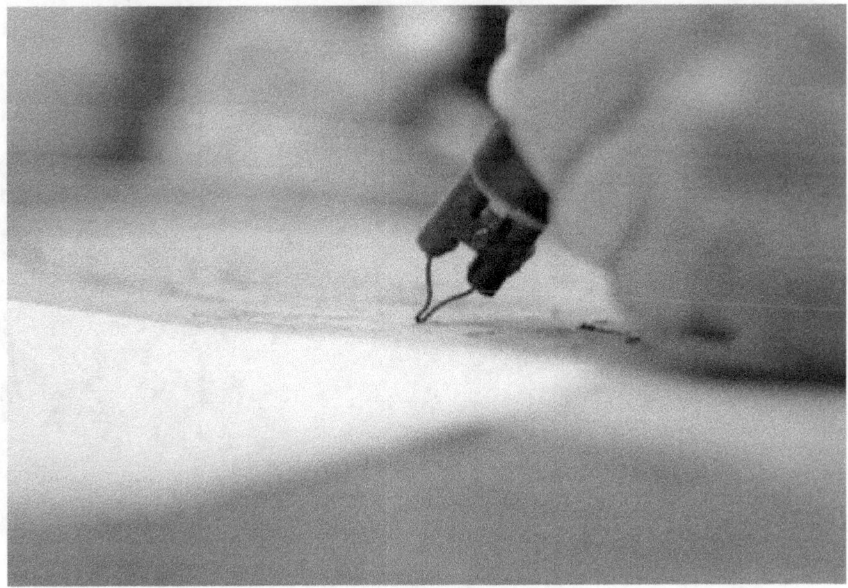

Another important consideration is to avoid pressing too hard with the tip so as to avoid prominent strokes that may unnecessarily dominate your artwork. Following a technique that uses light pressure helps to obtain consistent strokes. Gradual and medium pressure also helps you avoid mistakes and accidents when burning wood. Besides, the metal on wood burning tips tends to soften, and applying pressure at this point may bend the tip and make it ineffective for further use.

Applying steady pressure with your wood burning pen will help you achieve an evenly-etched effect throughout your design. It is also important to note that holding your wood burning pen longer in a specific area helps you achieve a darker and deeper effect. Further, to achieve the desired effect gradually, it is best to start wood burning along the outline or the edge of the wood. You may even want to burn the outline several times to achieve the required depth and color.

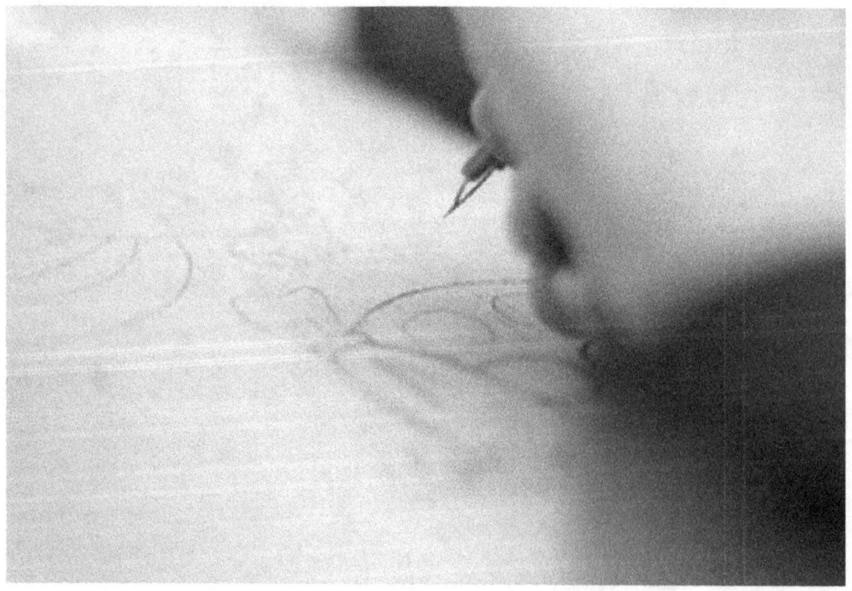

Finally, when working with designs that require changing direction frequently, a ball tip works best as it adheres to the surface of the wood, rather than sinking deep into it. For the same reason, ball tips offer more freedom when working with signboards, while other tips such as skew tips, chisel tips, and spear tips are useful for artwork that does not require you to change direction frequently.

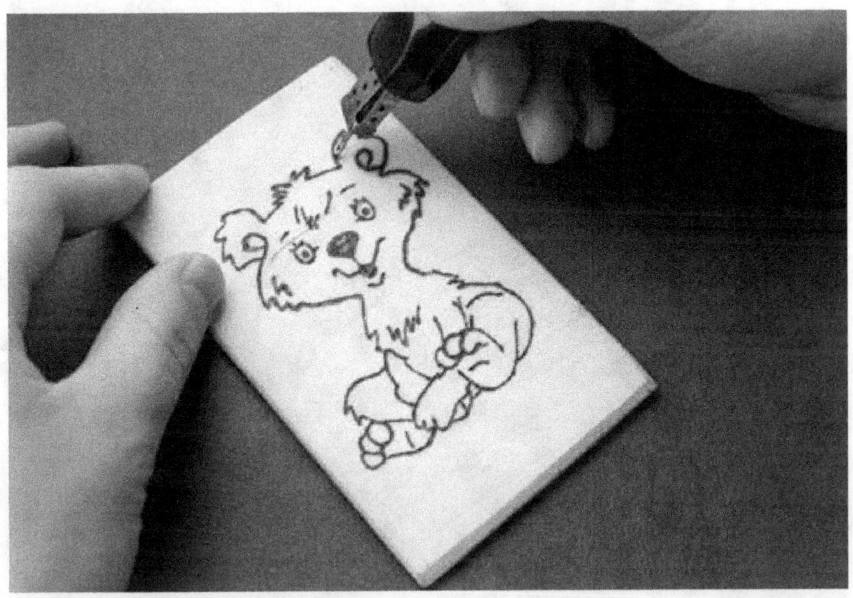

Even if you make small mistakes, try not to worry too much and continue to work with your design. You can easily correct most minor flaws by sanding or scraping them with a blade or a knife. This helps to get rid of the burnt wood to reveal fresh wood underneath. An important strategy to test the wood burning intensity of your pen is to use scrap wood. Using scrap wood allows you to understand how the heat from the tip will create an impression on your chosen piece of wood.

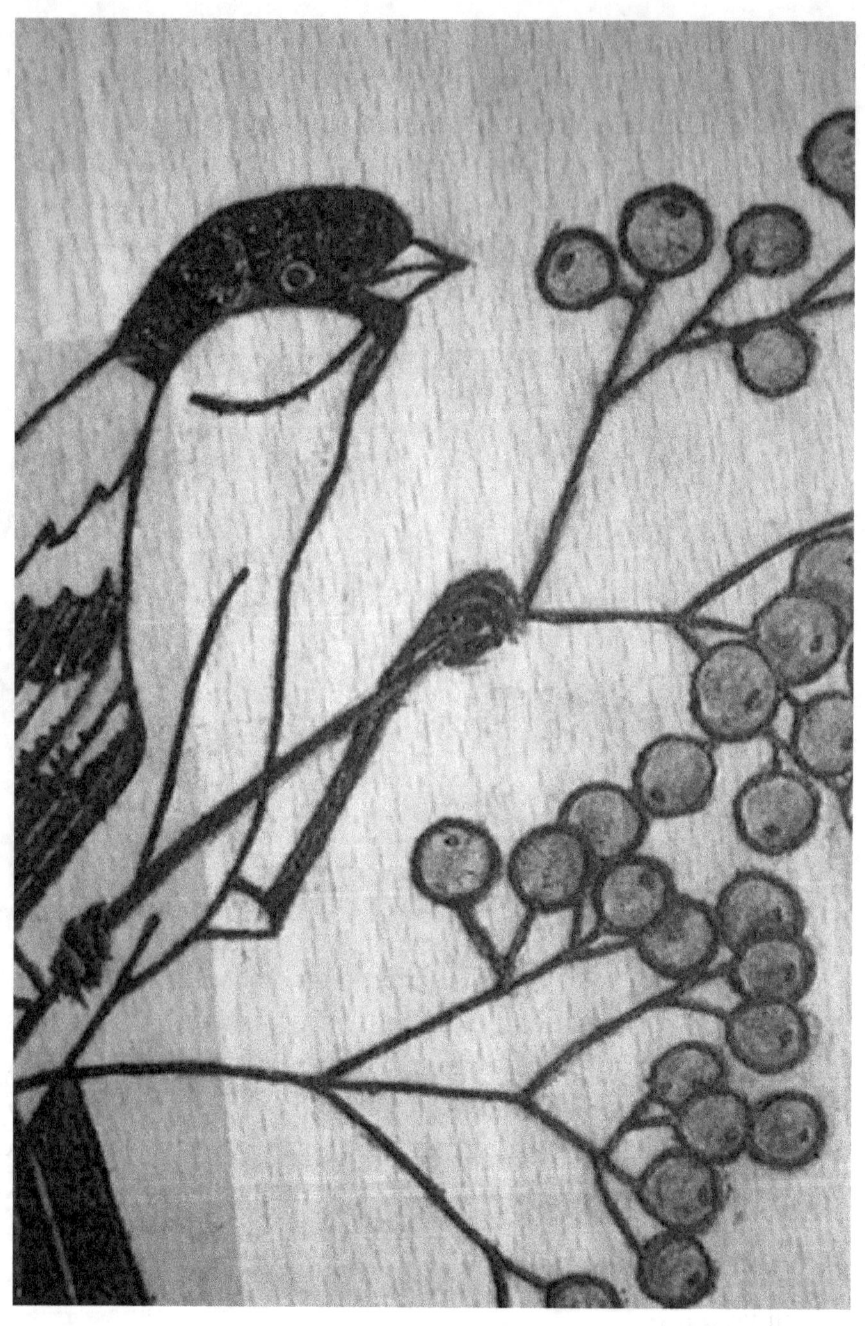

To produce stellar artwork, there are a few aspects you may want to incorporate into your pyrography practice.

First, as discussed before, softwood with less grain is more forgiving when compared to hard, grainy wood surfaces. Secondly, the wood burning pen gets quite hot and applying medium pressure when burning helps achieve an optimal design. Furthermore, when working with your wood burning pen, a small amount of residue often builds up on the top of its tip. This residue may be removed using sand paper (ideally 320 grit). It's best to use the sandpaper with a solid block to get rid of the residue. Another alternative is to use strop and aluminum oxide to remove the residue on the pen. To avoid any form of hazard when trying to remove residue from the heated pen tip, avoid holding onto the sandpaper for more than a second.

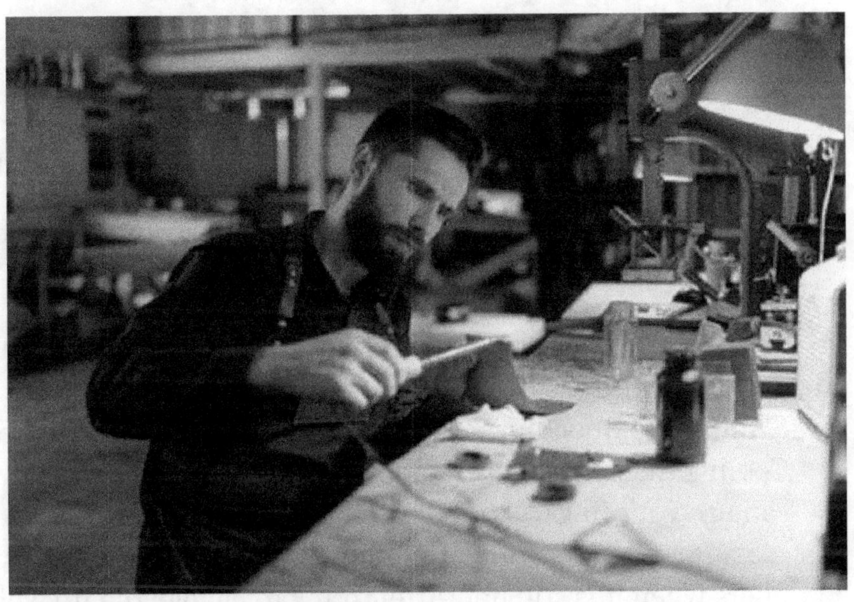

When changing tips, use pliers as the wood burning pens get extremely hot. After removing the tip, place it in a metal or glass dish to make sure it cools down gradually. It is also important to remember that even cool tips that you may want to replace must be handled using pliers as the barrel where they are supposed to be inserted tends to be hot.

Finally, your wood burning pen and all pyrography tools must be placed away from flammable materials and kept out of reach of children.

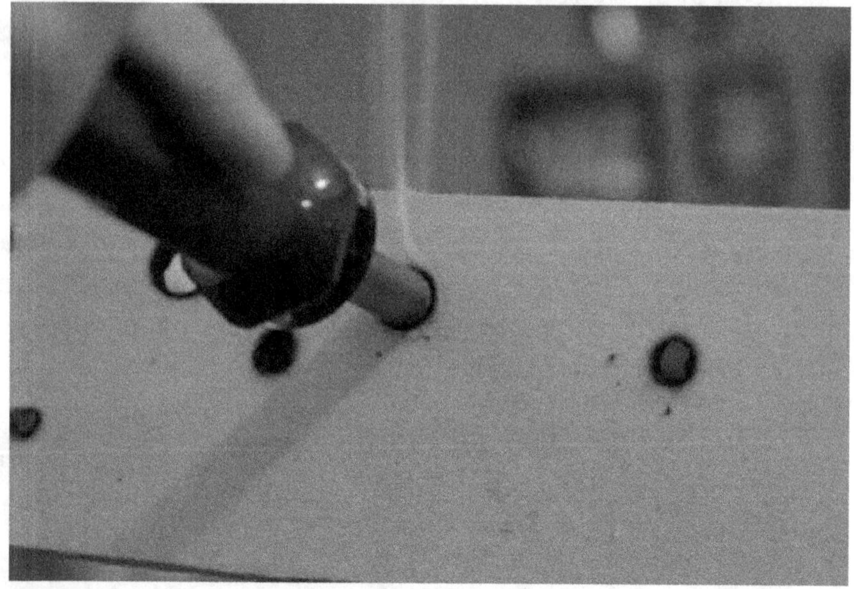

Important Considerations When Changing Tips for Wood Burning Pens

Typical wood burners may reach temperatures as high as 750-1050 degrees Fahrenheit or 450-565 degrees Celsius. Screw-style wood burners are equipped with soft brass tips. Cooling the pen requires about five minutes, after which you can use your fingers to remove the tip. It is not recommended that you attempt to change the tip even using pliers when it is still hot. Attempting to change the tip when the wood burner is hot may damage the threads present on the soft metal. In this context, it is worth mentioning that you can comfortably replace the handle of a wire-nib burner with the tip/pen combination even when it is hot. For projects that require you to change tips every now and then, this feature provides a high level of convenience.

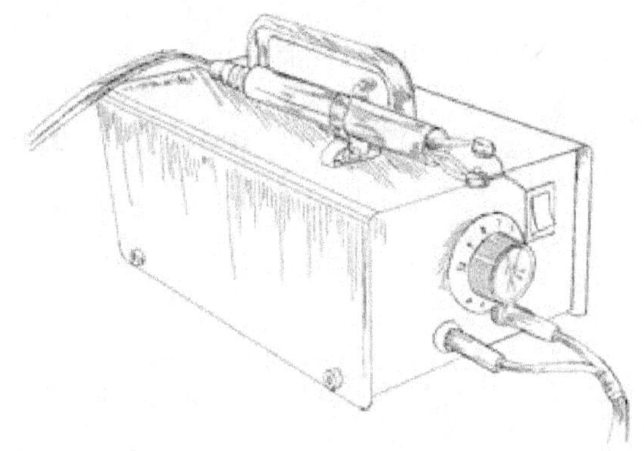

Chapter Summary

- It is essential to know how to use a wood burner to produce professional pyrography artwork.

- Wood burning tips have gauges - the thicker the wire, the smaller the gauge.

- Wire-nib have different gauges to achieve the desired effect: spear tip (pointed edge), skew tip (slanted tip), round tip (circular point),chisel tip (perpendicular burn edges), ballpoint tip (ball attached to the end).

- The solid-point burner may be used by one of the following tips: universal tip (suitable for burning outlines), extra-fine tip (suitable for curves and lines), shading tip (suitable for a shading effect), and calligraphy tip (drawing curved lines).

- General tips for pyrography artwork are included below:

- Hold the wood burning pen like you would hold a pen, but take care not to hold it against the wood for too long.

- Use a "landing - take off" maneuver to progress with your pyrography artwork.

- To darken an area, use gradual, circular strokes on medium heat.

- Work in the direction of the wood grain for best results.

- Use light pressure for consistent strokes throughout.

- Avoid pressing too hard with the pen tip to avoid prominent strokes.

- Use ball tips for designs that change direction frequently, such as preparing signboards.

- Correct minor mistakes by scraping with a blade.

- Remember that the wood burning pen can get quite hot.

- Remove the residue that builds on your pen tip periodically to produce tidy artwork.

- Use pliers to change tips even when the tip is cold as the barrel where the tips goes may be too hot.

- Keep your pyrography kit and materials away from children and inflammable materials.

Points to remember when changing wood burning tips:

- Burners reach very high temperatures, as much as 750-1050 degrees Fahrenheit or 450-565 degrees Celsius.

- Allow the pen to cool for at least five minutes before you attempt to touch its tip.

- It is not recommended to change tips for the screw-style burners when they are too hot even with a pliers as its threads may get damaged.

- Tips for Wire-nib burners can be changed even when they are hot. For the same reason, wire-nib burners are suitable for projects that require you to change tips often.

In the next chapter you will learn how to make your own wood burning tool using simple objects such as syringe needles and USB cable.

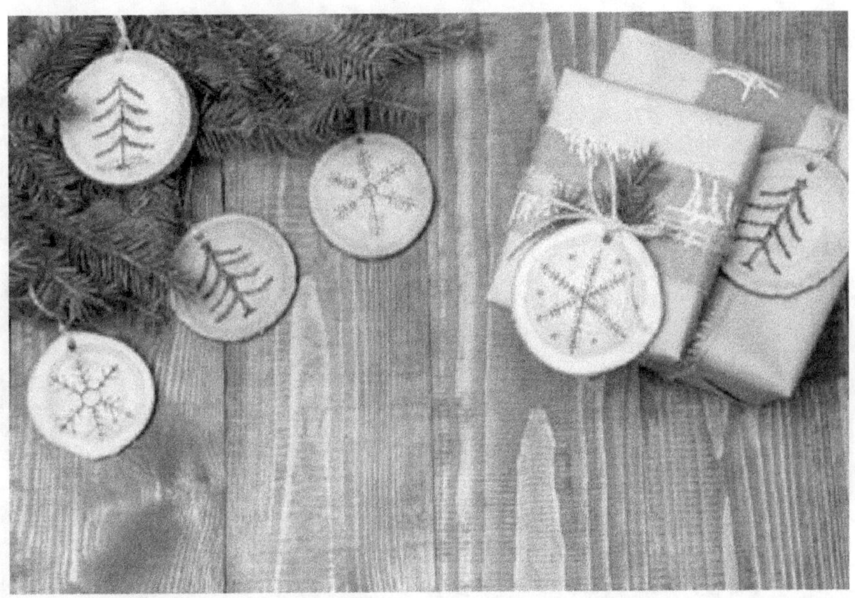

Chapter Four:
How to Make Your Own Wood Burning Tool

The best way to start mastering the art of pyrography is to build your own USB pyro-pen. The USB pyro-pen is a simple tool that can be easily heated using a USB power source. You will need the following items to build your own USB pyro-pen.

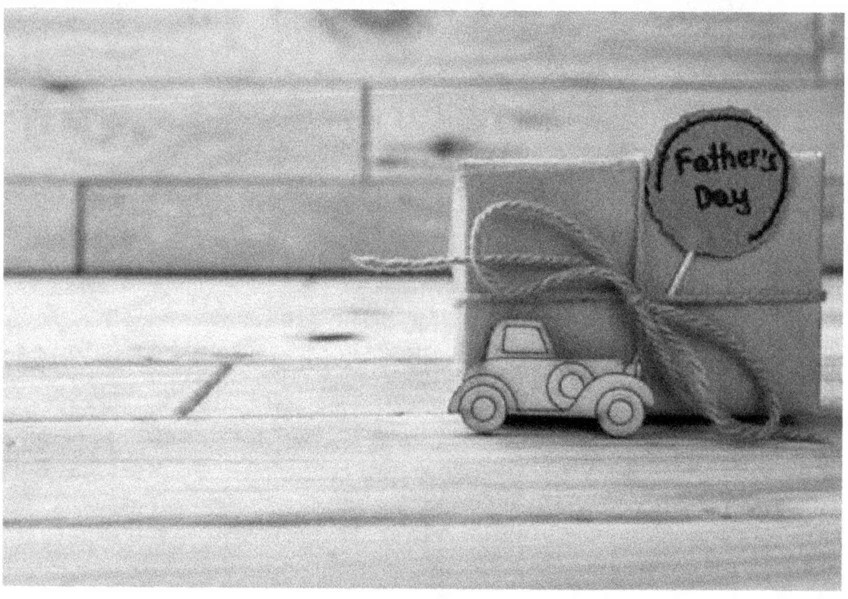

- *Two Syringes* - You may get any type of disposable syringes from a pharmacy. To build your project, you will only require the needles to craft a burn tip for your customized wood burning tool.

- *Pliers* - You will also need pliers as it is a versatile hand tool to hold hot objects as well as bend metals.

In your project, you will use the pliers to bend the needle to the desired shape for burning wood.

- *Electric Tape* - An electric Tape can effectively insulate any type of wire that conducts electricity. Electric tapes follow a colour coding system and a black electric tape serves as an insulator. Using an electric tape for your wood burning tool makes it safe to use.

- *Common Thread* - You will need thread to wrap your wood burning tool and secure the tip in place. A standard black thread is used in this demonstration. However, any other colour also serves the purpose.

- *Super Glue* - Super glue is a fast-bonding adhesive with high strength. It instantly secures the surfaces to which it is applied. It is resistant to shock, vibration, and other environmental damage. Super glue is essential to make a durable wood burning tool. It can secure the different components of the tool even when a high temperature is applied and helps achieve the desired artistic effect on wood.

- *Rectangular Wooden Block* - You will require a wooden block, preferably a long rectangular block, to practice your wood burning skills or design your first pyrography project.

- *USB Cable* - A USB cable is modified for the project to conveniently connect the wood burning tool to a standard power source using a DC charger.

- *Scissors* - You will also need scissors to cut the USB cable, thread, and electric tape and build a sleek, hand-made customized wood burning tool.

- *Power Brick* -A power brick will be used to connect the wood burning tool to the power source.

When you have the required materials and components, it is time to start building your wood burning tool. The following steps will help you design an effective tool with a skew tip.

- *Detach the Needles* - This project does not require the use of the barrel and plunger. Rather, you will just need the needle. A syringe needle is secured in its hub. Since you are going to need only the needle, use a pliers to hold the needle and carefully pull it out of its hub.

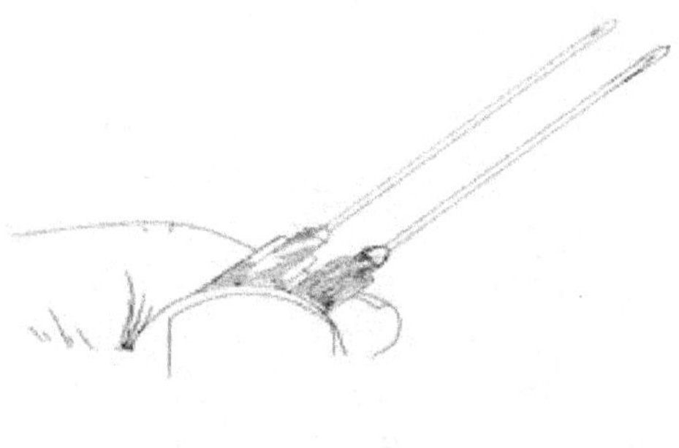

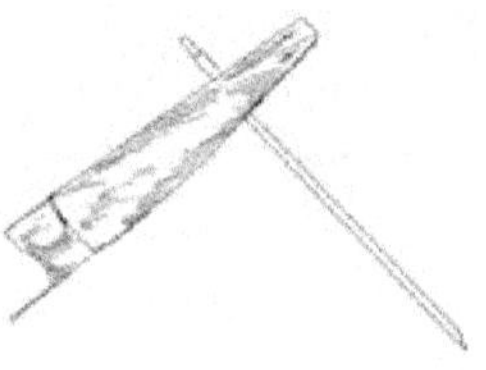

- *Connect the USB Cable to the Needles* - Your next step is to cut the USB cable and attach it to the needles. You can use any standard USB charging cable that comes with most smartphones or mobile phones. Cut the smaller end of the USB cable that has the connector which goes into the charging point of your smartphone.

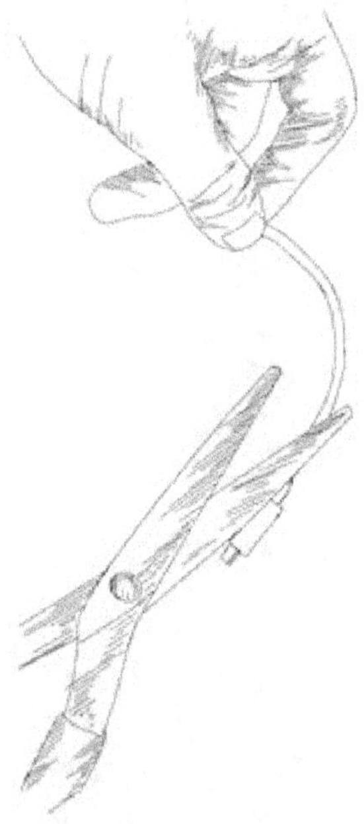

Now cut across the sheath vertically, taking care not to damage the wires inside. Pull back the shielding to reveal the wires.

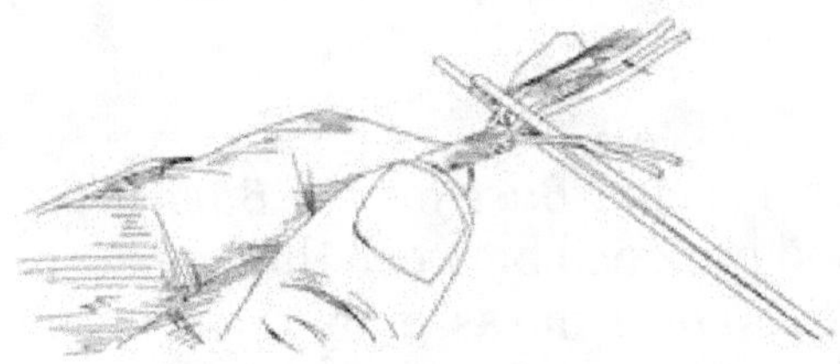

You will find four coloured wires - green, white, red, and black. The green and white wires are used for data transfer, and the read and black wires are the power wires. Pull back the green and white wires and remove the insulating sheath only for the red and black wires. This will expose their tips.

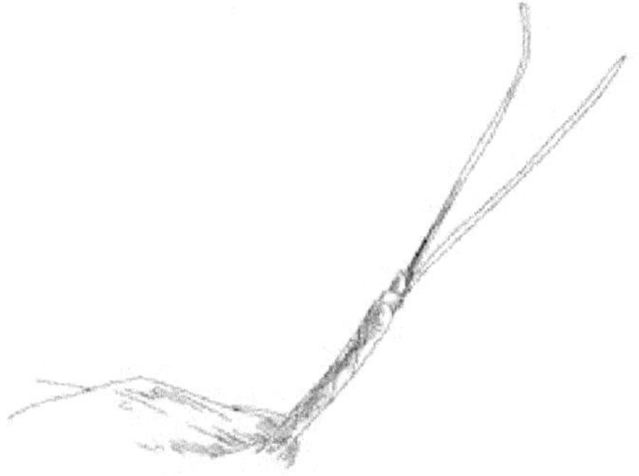

Now connect the needles to the tips of the wires.

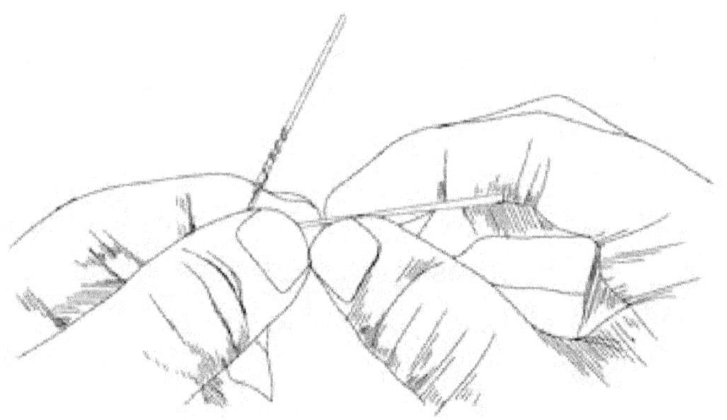

- *Create a Secure Base for the Burn Tip* - Place a piece of wood or pencil between the two needles and wrap the thread over the assembly.

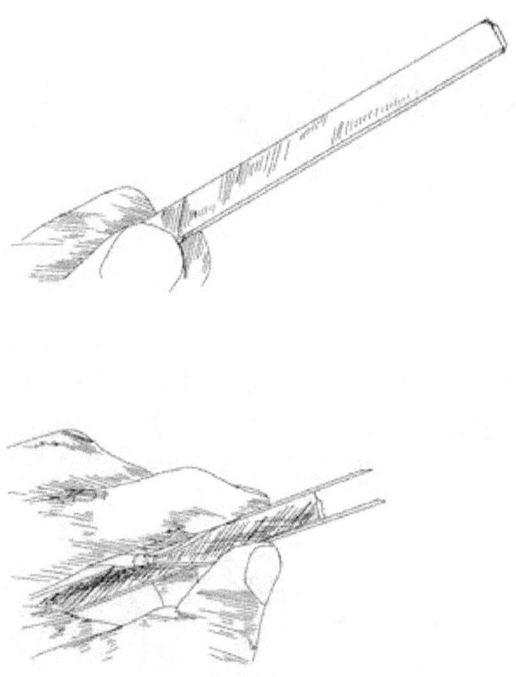

Wrap a large length of the thread until it covers an inch of the space and you can no longer see the piece of wood where you wrapped the thread.

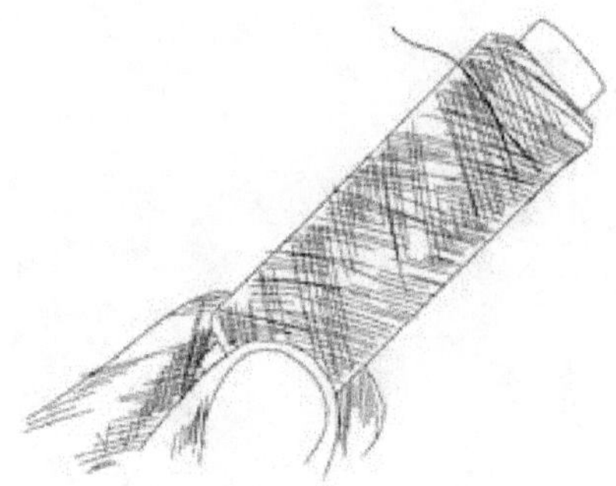

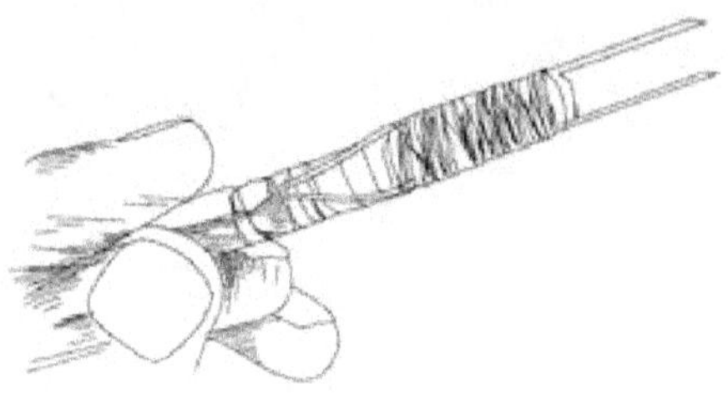

Next, apply the superglue liberally all over the thread to stick it to the piece of wood between the needles.

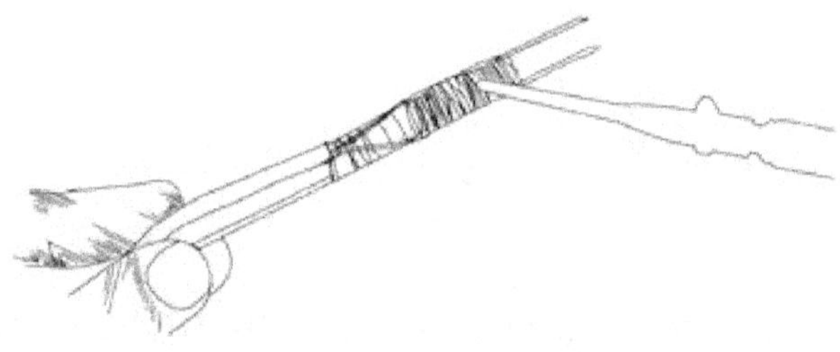

Thereafter, wrap the black electric tape over the base of the burn tip.

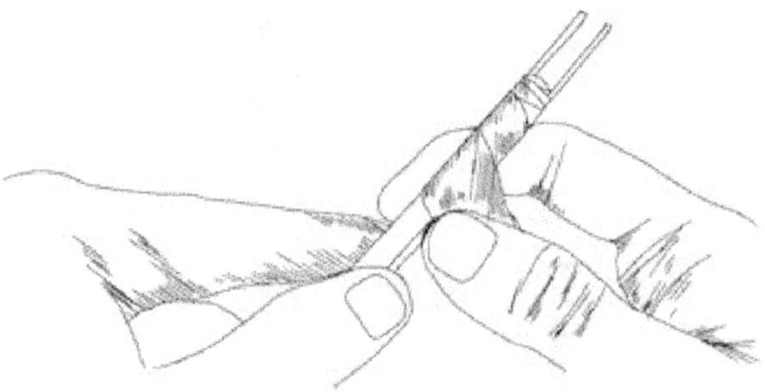

Now you have a neat black base with insulation for your burn tip.

- *Craft the Needle Tip* - Use pliers to bend one of the needles at a slanted angle so that it rests on the other needle.

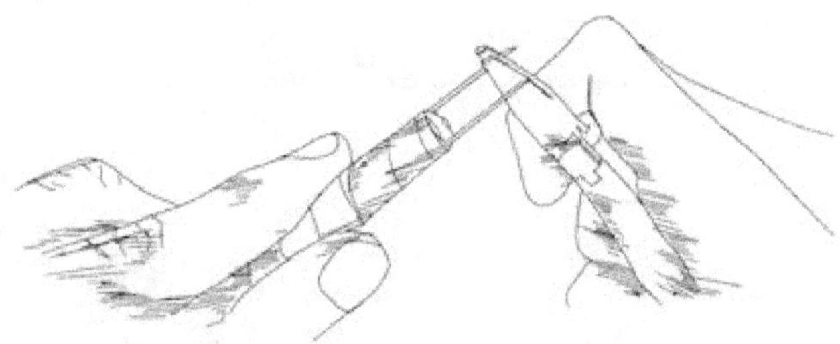

Eventually, it should resemble a skew tip as in the case of wire-nib needle tips described in the previous chapter.

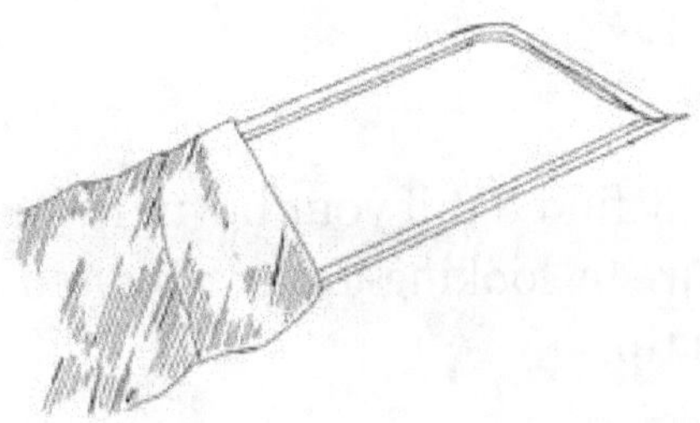

- *Heat the Burn Tip* - Your customized burn tip is now ready to use. Connect the other end of the USB cable into the power brick and plug it into the wall socket to start heating your wire nib.

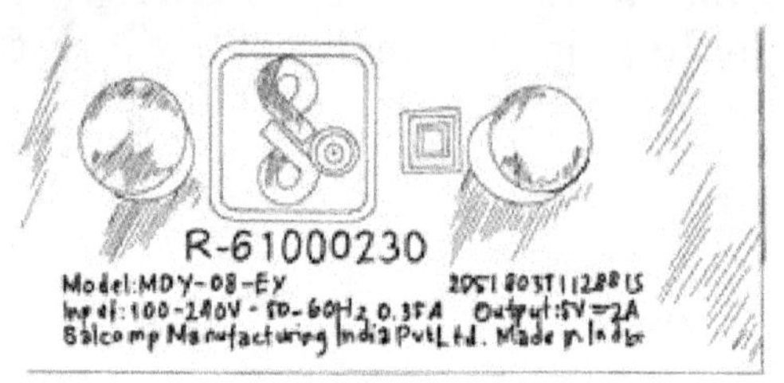

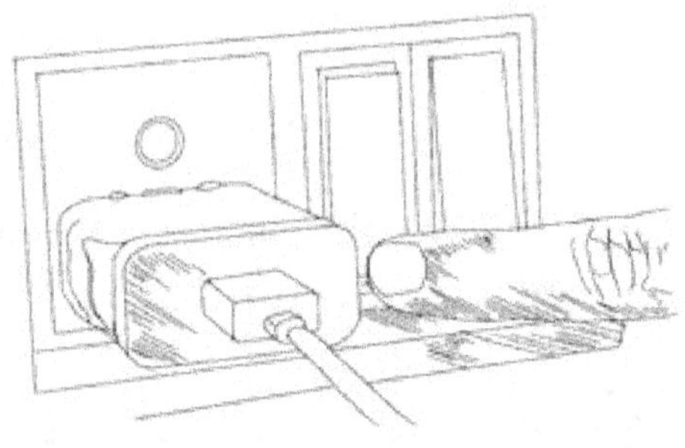

You may find out if your burn tip has reached the desired temperature by looking for a red colour at the bent angle of your burn tip.

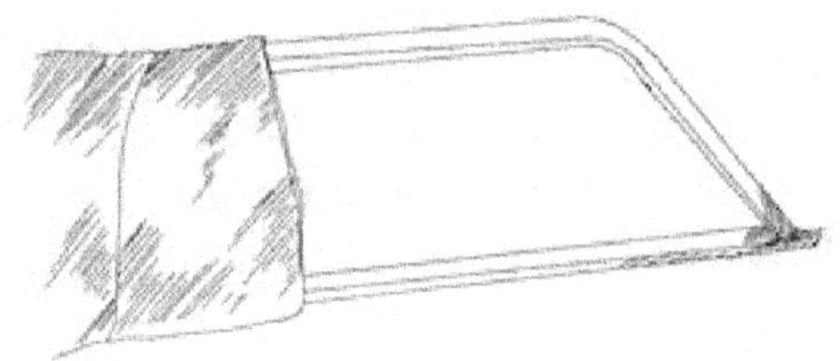

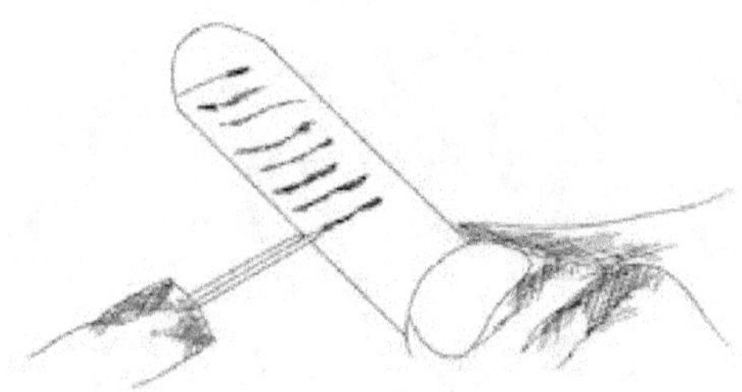

Chapter Summary

- Building your own USB pyro-pen is is simple and fun.

- The tip is created from two syringe needles.

- The tip is held in place using a piece of wood, secured with common thread, bonded with super glue, and insulated with electric tape.

- The burn tip is heated by connecting the power leads of the USB cable to the two needle ends.

In the next chapter you will learn how to draw straight and curved lines, meandering lines, waves, and apply shading to your pyrography artwork.

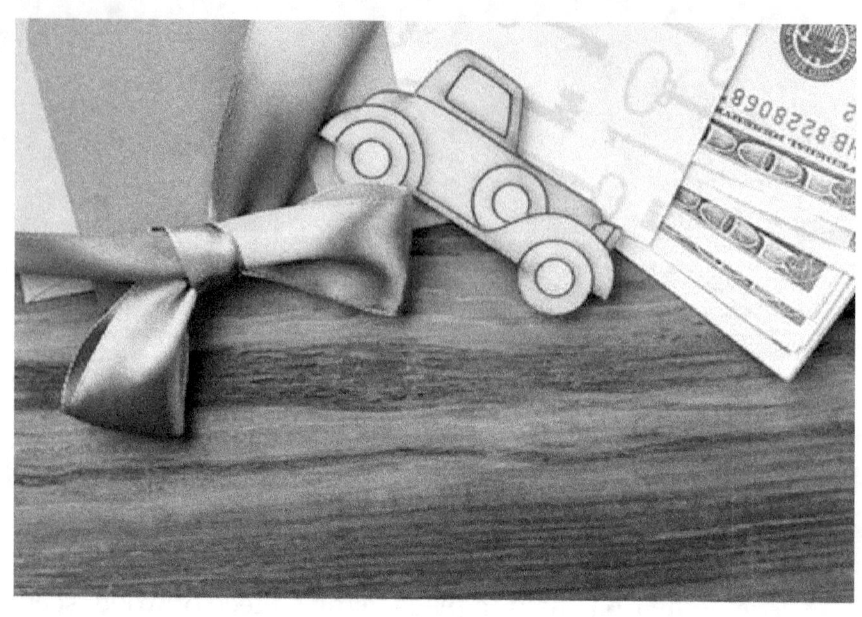

Chapter Five: Basic Line Techniques for Wood Burning

Learning the right wood burning technique is essential to successfully incorporating a high level of detail in your artwork. Applying the right pyrography technique is the first step to effortlessly drawing on wood, and finally achieving flawless 3D art.

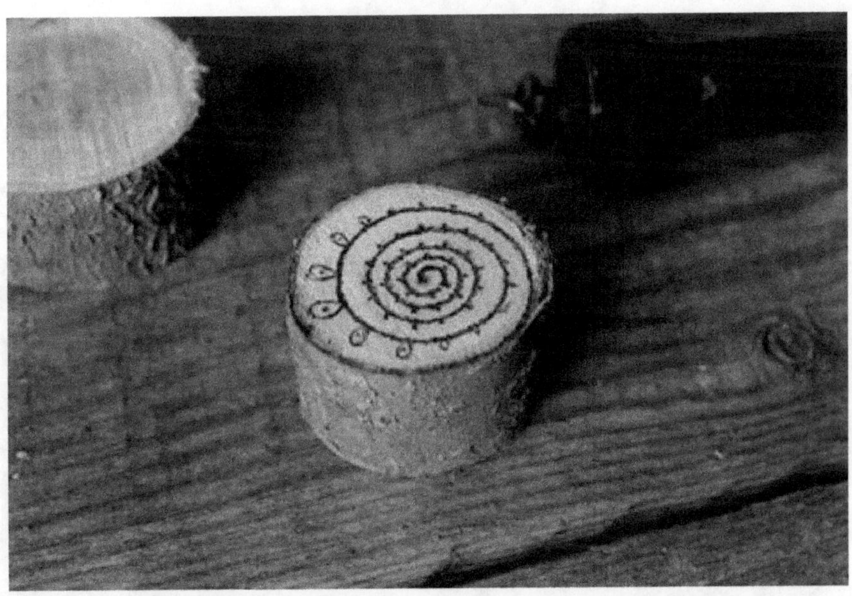

Any pyrography project requires basic skills to burn different types of strokes on wood.

- *Straight Lines* – To draw straight lines, burn two points, and then burn a line which is the shortest distance between the two points. You may use either the tip of the nib or the edge of the nib to burn the line on wood. It is possible to burn thin lines or darker lines by changing the pressure applied on the wood. The figure below illustrates this.

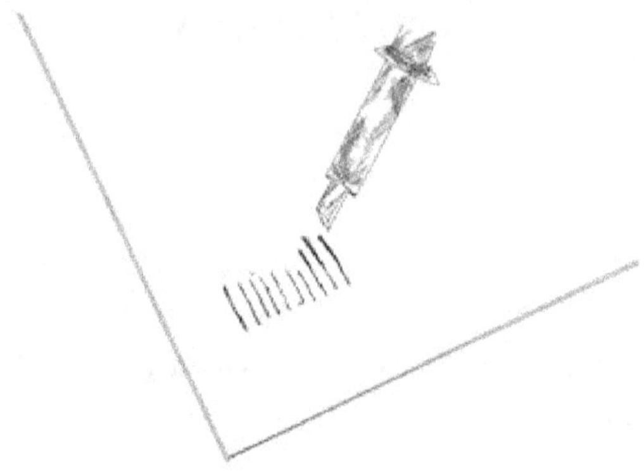

- *Curve* – Apply similar pressure to burn a curve using the tip of the nib attached to your burn tool. Trace a curve several times to understand how you can get a perfect curve without blobs. Blobs occur when you rest the burn tip at the same spot for a long time. You may also try to create a curve in the reverse direction to identify which direction is most comfortable and produces a perfect curve. It is also a great idea to practice doing different types of curves such as shallow curves and deep curves.

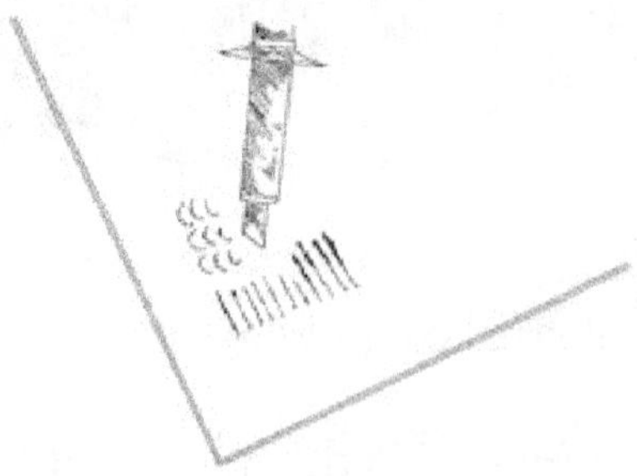

It is interesting to note how an entirely different effect is created when using the edge of the tool to draw the curve.

The start of the curve produces an accent and the curve ends with a heavy line. Understanding the effects produced on applying different degrees of pressure to obtain the desired curve on wood helps you choose the right strategy to produce your desired artwork.

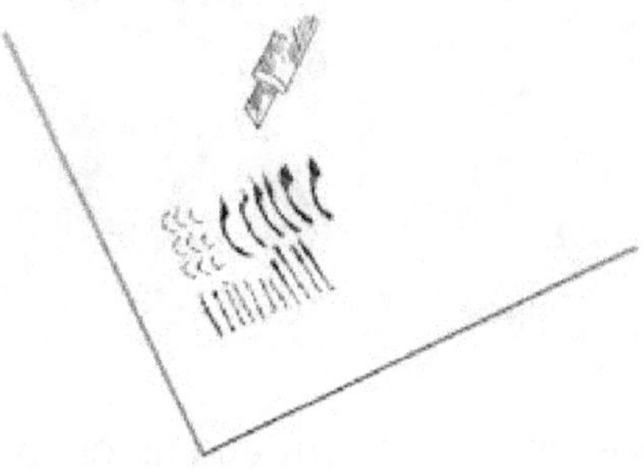

- *Dotted Lines* – You may obtain dotted lines by applying light pressure with the tip of your wood burning tool. Varying the pressure and duration when applying the burn tip on wood helps you achieve thin dots or heavy dots.

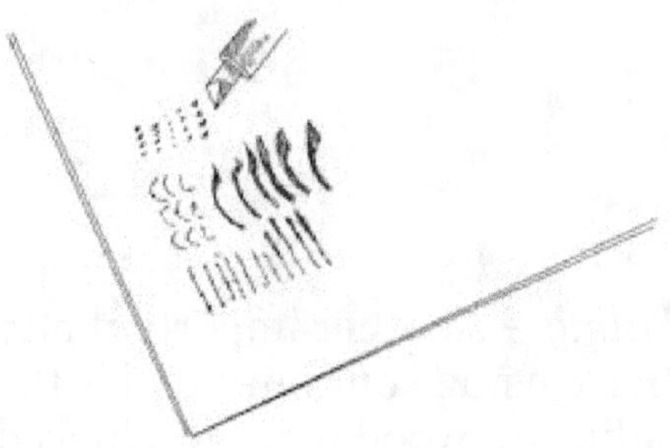

- *Meandering Lines* – Your next exercise is to burn curvy meandering lines with the burn tip to get a feel of the interaction between the burn tip and the wood surface. You will also understand how varying pressure achieves a different type of effect on the wood surface.

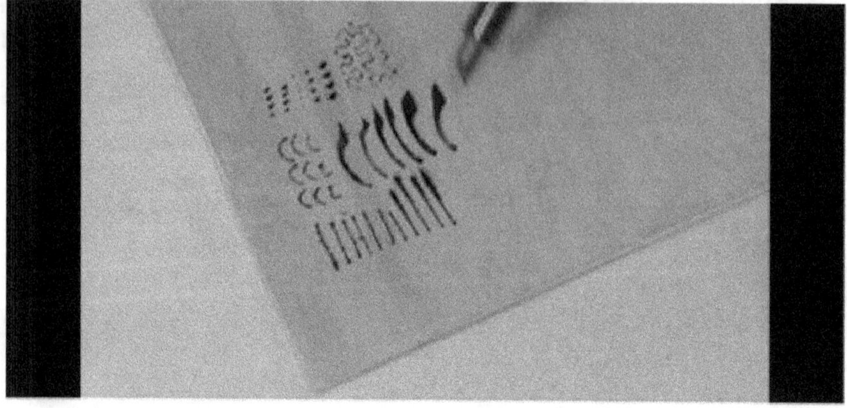

- *Waves* – Waves are much easier to achieve than meandering lines. Waves may also be achieved using the tip of your burn tool.

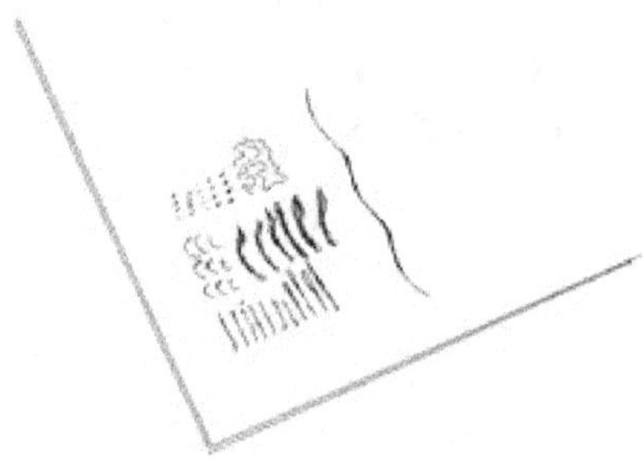

- *Shading* – Another important effect that you can achieve using your burn tool is the shading effect. Shading on wood may be achieved by using the edge of your burn tool and applying very gentle pressure to obtain different colors on the wood. Applying less pressure helps you achieve light shades and more pressure achieves darker shades on wood.

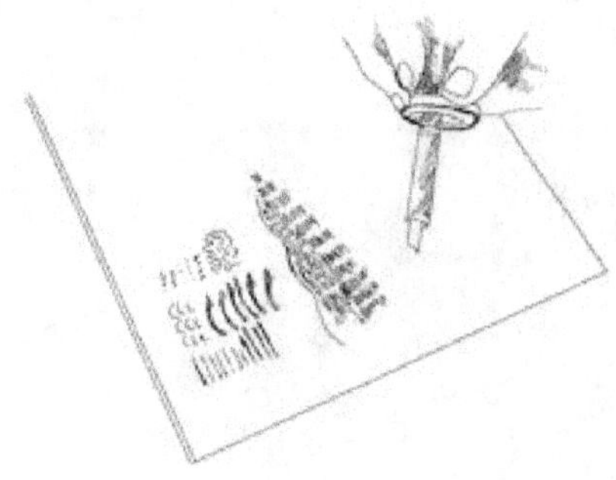

More on Achieving Different Effects with Shading in Wood

To start with, filling may be achieved with a flat gradient tip on large surfaces. When working with small surfaces, a calligraphy pen proves useful. You may set the temperature setting on medium to high heat for best results. Avoid using too much heat as you may be tempted into thinking that doing so achieves faster results. On the contrary, applying a large amount of heat may cause unwanted stroke marks on your artwork.

Working soft circular movements on medium heat, gradually darkening the area, helps to achieve the right shading effect. Another rule of thumb is that applying more heat creates a higher level of opacity. Furthermore, working with the right temperature setting helps to obtain the right contrast.

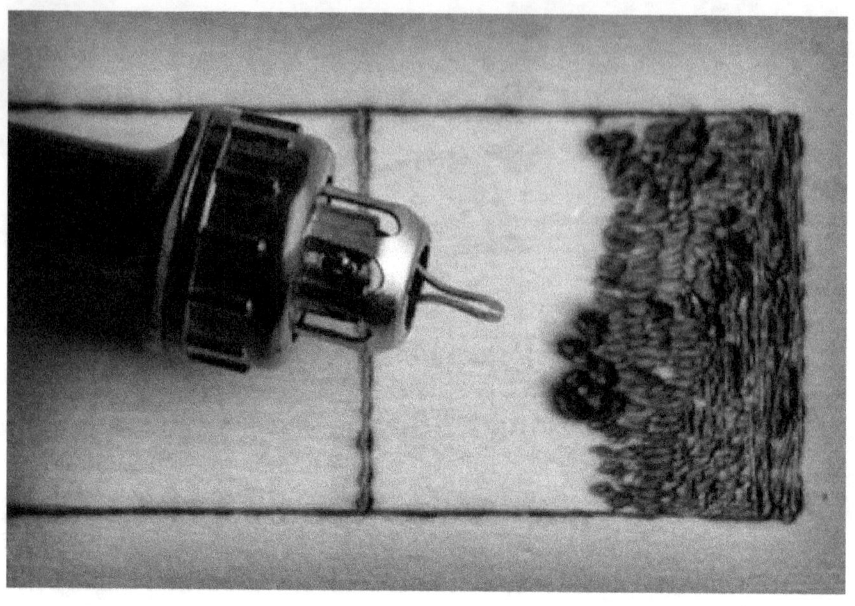

You can achieve finer gradients by working slowly and with less heat, such as a 4 or 5 setting on a scale of 10 for the wood burning tool. A flat tip may be used to achieve the desired gradients. Note that shading does not appear immediately. It is visible only after completing a few circular movements over a specific area. A good practice in shading is to work with adjacent areas as opposed to distant areas, as the former are already warm and more receptive to heat.

When using gradients, the grain in the wood is hardest to work with. Gradients are not clearly visible with large grains. However, you may be able to achieve the right tone by applying more heat.

Another useful technique to achieve a shading effect is to use hatches and cross-hatches. The technique is especially effective when the wood contains grain.

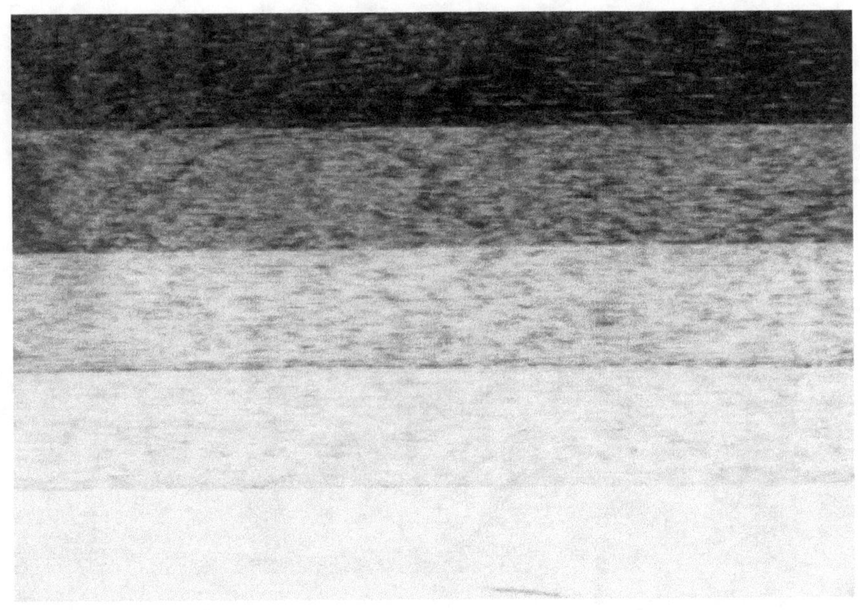

Shading techniques also help you achieve the desired textures. A flat shading tip may be used on high heat to achieve a hair-like effect. Applying more pressure gives darker strokes, and subtle pressure gives soft shades. While defining an area, you can leave some spaces blank to represent lighting.

Further, a fur-like effect may be achieved using a round or sharp tip. Darker fur may be achieved by defining strokes close together on high heat. On the other hand, soft fur is achieved using faster strokes with more spacing. You may even create a cracking-skin-effect by using a flat tip to achieve dark edges.

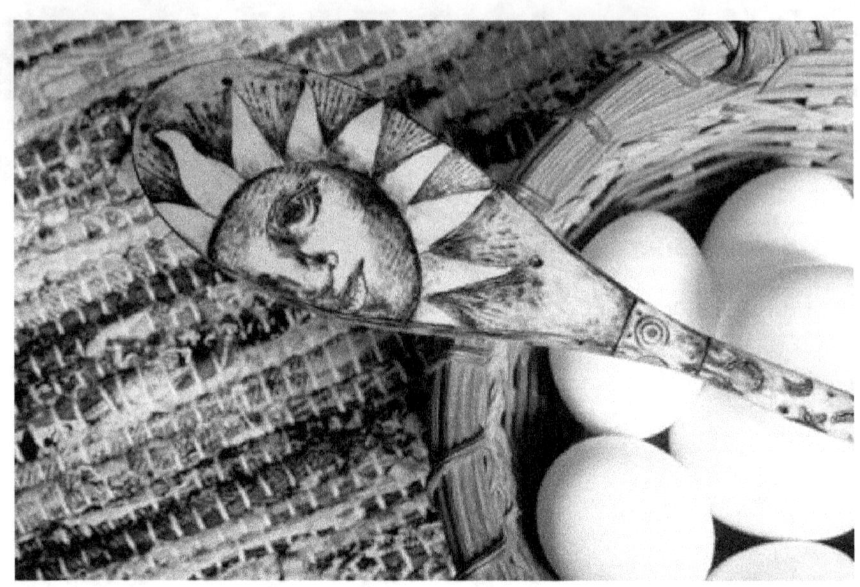

Chapter Summary

- To apply a high level of impressive detail in your pyrography artwork, it is essential you learn basic line art and shading techniques. To give your pyrography artwork an impressive look, you need to understand how to draw basic lines using the tip and edge of your wood burning tool:

    o You can draw straight lines by burning two points, and then burning a line between them. You could burn the line either with the tip of the nib or edge of your burn tool.

    o Varying thickness may be achieved for the lines by varying the level of pressure applied on the wood.

    o To draw a curve, you could use the tip of the nib to trace a curvy line. Practice in the forward and reverse direction to achieve smooth curves. Also practice shallow and deep curves to achieve best results with pyrography artwork.

- o   When the edge of the burn tool is used to burn a curve in wood, it creates an accent at the beginning of the curve and a heavy end, similar to what you would achieve with a calligraphy pen.

- o   Dotted lines may be drawn using the tip of your burn tool. Vary the intensity and duration of pressure applied to achieve thin and heavy dots.

- o   You could also practice meandering lines with the tip of your burn tool to get better control over the basic maneuvers in pyrography.

- o   It is also possible to create waves with the tip of your burn tool.

- Shading and gradients are the most vivid effects you could achieve with the edge of your burn tool.

- o   Shading is generally achieved by applying gentle pressure.

- o   Less pressure gives lighter shades, whereas more pressure gives darker shades.

- o   Practice shading using the edge of your burn tool.

- o   Work with soft circular movements to achieve the right shading effect.

- o   The flat tip is most useful when shading by burning wood.

- o   Vary the temperature to achieve different shades, level of opacity, and contrast.

- o   Avoid very high temperatures as it may create stroke marks on wood

- Gradients are hard to achieve with large grains. Applying more heat helps to achieve the right tone for gradients.

- Work with hatches and cross-hatches to achieve gradients where grain is present in the wood.

- You may also achieve textures by burning wood, such as the fur-like effect and the cracking skin effect.

In the next chapter you will learn how to use stencils to make designs and patterns.

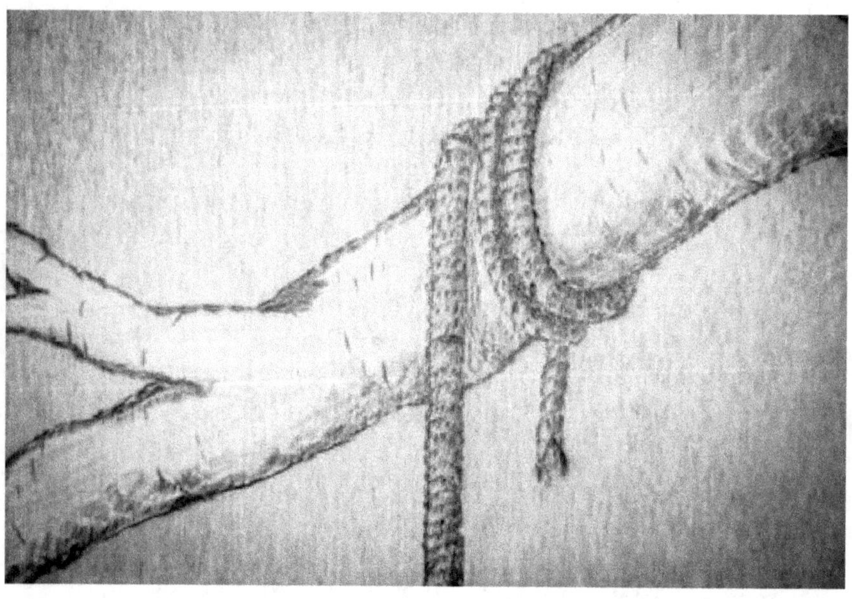

Chapter Six: Making Patterns and Designs with the Use of Stencils

Stencils help you create beautiful patterns using the pyrography technique. Stencils are useful tools as they help define a flawless pattern in wood. Stencils are perfect for creative projects and a wide variety of decorative templates are available at most stores with a physical location or online presence.

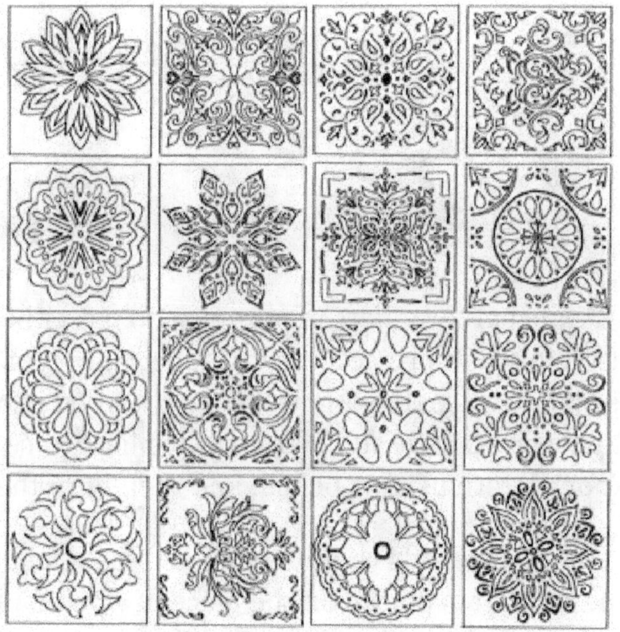

Many pyrography professionals rely on number and letter stencils to achieve good results with burning text on wood. Stencils help achieve the right spacing between characters and provide a consistent size throughout the wood burning project.

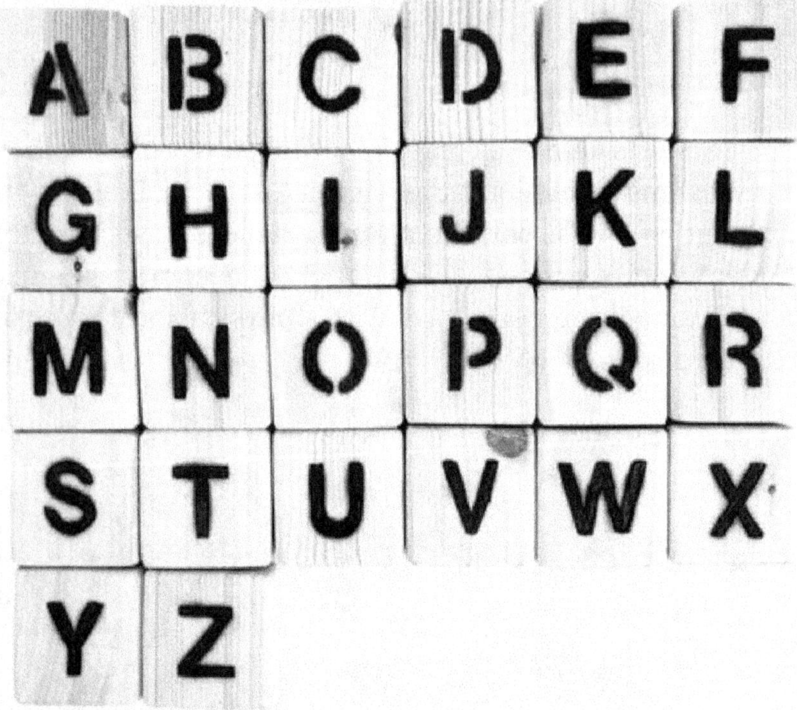

While pyrographers may choose to use either metal or plastic for their projects, metal stencils are preferred as it is possible to trace them on wood with a wood burning tool. When using plastic stencils, pyrographers trace the required text or pattern using a pencil, and then burn the pattern.

A metal stencil is a thin stainless steel sheet (usually 0.3 mm thick). It is placed on the piece of wood directly and burnt using the desired burn tip of a wood burning tool.

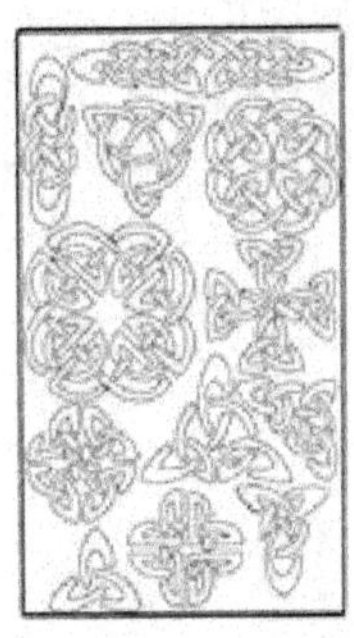 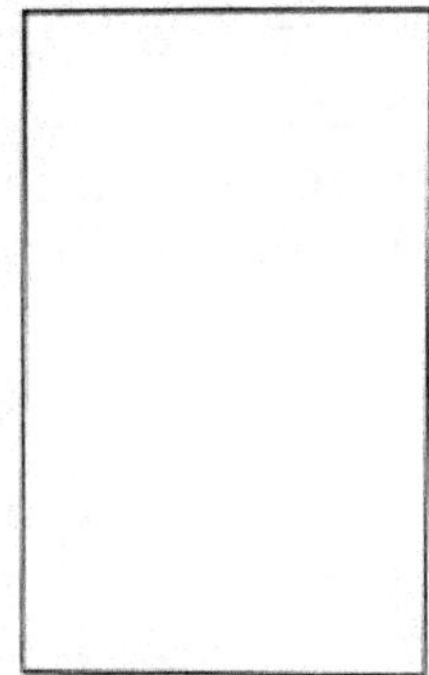

As you continue to burn the wood beneath your metal stencil, the stencil may get hot and start lifting off from the wood surface. It may even bend when exposed to the heat. In such cases, it is essential to let the metal cool down before you proceed with your artwork. When the metal lifts off from your piece of wood, and you continue to burn the wood, you may not be able to achieve the desired result. Your pattern may be distorted and you may not be able to achieve the required spacing. Therefore, it is best to let the metal stencil cool off before you proceed to burn the rest of the design. In most cases, a pattern may be far easier to trace when compared to tracing letters and numbers since letter placement requires consistent spacing.

When struggling with letter and number spacing, it is best to trace the required sequence of characters with a pencil and then proceed to burn the pattern with a stencil.

A step-by-step guide to burning the desired design on wood using a metal stencil is described below:

- *Choose a Stencil that Fits Your Requirements* – Pick a desired pattern in metal that will help you achieve the desired artwork on wood. Make your wood ready for burning by using a sandpaper to smooth it out in the direction of the grain, and wipe it with a clean cloth or cheesecloth. You may want to attach the desired tip to your wood burning tool at this point. When you are ready, plug in your tool to heat it up.

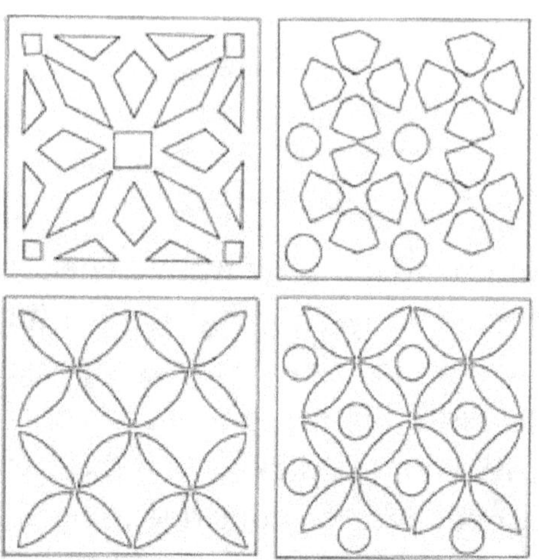

- *Place your Metal Stencil on the Wood* – To place the metal stencil on wood, you may place a graphite paper on wood, and then place the stencil over it. ALternatively, upi may place the stencil directly on the surface of wood. When using graphite paper, you may want to tape it onto the wood so it does not slip as you burn the design.

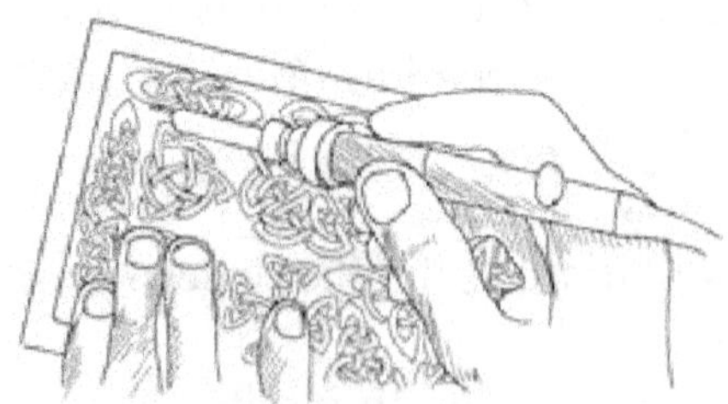

- *Start Burning your Desired Pattern* – Hold your wood burning tool as you would hold your pencil. Detailed information on holding and working with your wood tool and it's different tips is described in "Chapter 3" on tips and techniques on using wood burners. First trace the outside of the stencil on the graphite paper so the design is engraved on wood. You may want to erase lines when transferring the design with the graphite paper.

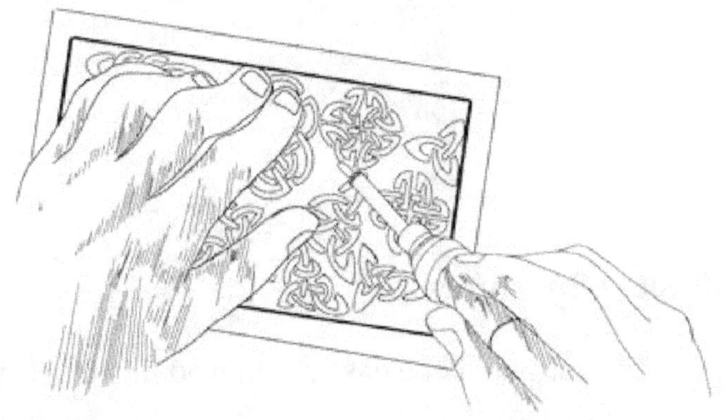

When burning wood by placing the stencil directly on the wood, place the stencil sturdily. Do not move the stencil and start burning the pattern on wood. To avoid moving the stencil when you are still burning the design, move the wooden block along with the stencil to get a better grip.

Things to Remember when you are Burning Wood

It is important to maintain a constant heat throughout the process and apply constant pressure throughout the wood burning process. As mentioned before, make sure you let the metal stencil cool off whenever you find that it has been bent or lifted off the wood due to the heat applied by the wood burning tool. When you are finished with your artwork, slowly lift your stencil and your desired pattern is ready. To give your artwork the final finishing touch, you may use colors and varnish or a wood finish to seal your design.

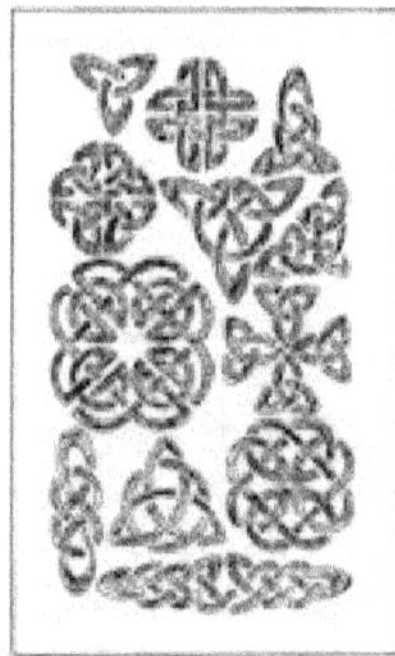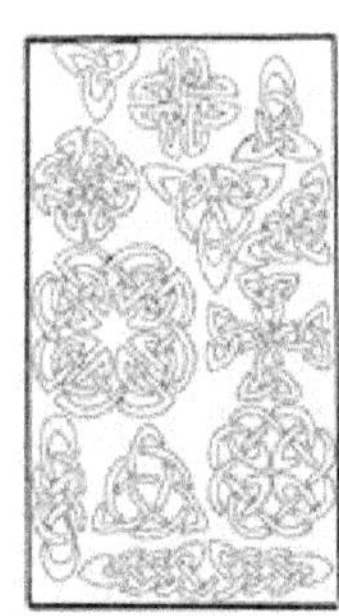

Chapter Summary

- Patterns may be easily achieved in pyrography using stencils.

- Stencils help create flawless, creative, and decorative patterns in wood.

- Number and letter stencils are widely used by pyrography professionals.

- Stencils are available in metal and plastic, although metal stencils (0.3mm thick stainless steel sheets) are preferred over wood.

- You may use the tip of the wood burning tool to burn areas defined by the stencil.

- When the stencil gets hot, remember to allow it to cool as it may lift off the wood surface or bend, and distort your artwork.

- Letter and number stencils may be traced to achieve the desired spacing and consistent design before burning the pattern.

A step-by-step process of burning wood using stencils is summarized below:

- Smooth out the wood using sandpaper in the direction of the grain and wipe it off with a clean cloth.

- Attach the desired burn tip and heat your burn tool.

- Place the metal stencil on wood. Optionally, you may use graphite paper on the wood prior to placing the stencil.

- Hold the wood burning tool sturdily and start burning the pattern.

- Do not move the stencil. Instead, move the whole block of wood to get a better grip.

- Remember to apply constant pressure.

- Add finishing touches to the design by applying wood polish or varnish.

In the next chapter you will learn how to transfer images to wood and add that professional touch to your artwork.

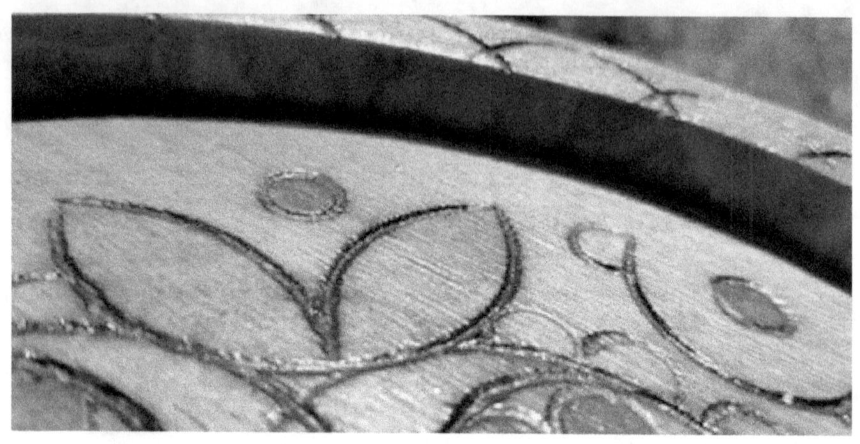

Chapter Seven:
Image Transfer Techniques

Transferring an image into wood is the best way to incorporate a professional touch in your artwork. It is easy to find an image outline that resonates with your design. The basic steps to transfer your printed pattern on wood are listed below.

- Start with the desired printed image.

- Place the printed artwork over a carbon paper on your piece of wood.

- Trace the outline of the image on the wood.

- Burn the imprinted design with a wood burning tool. Use the desired burning or shading technique to get the perfect photography impression on wood.

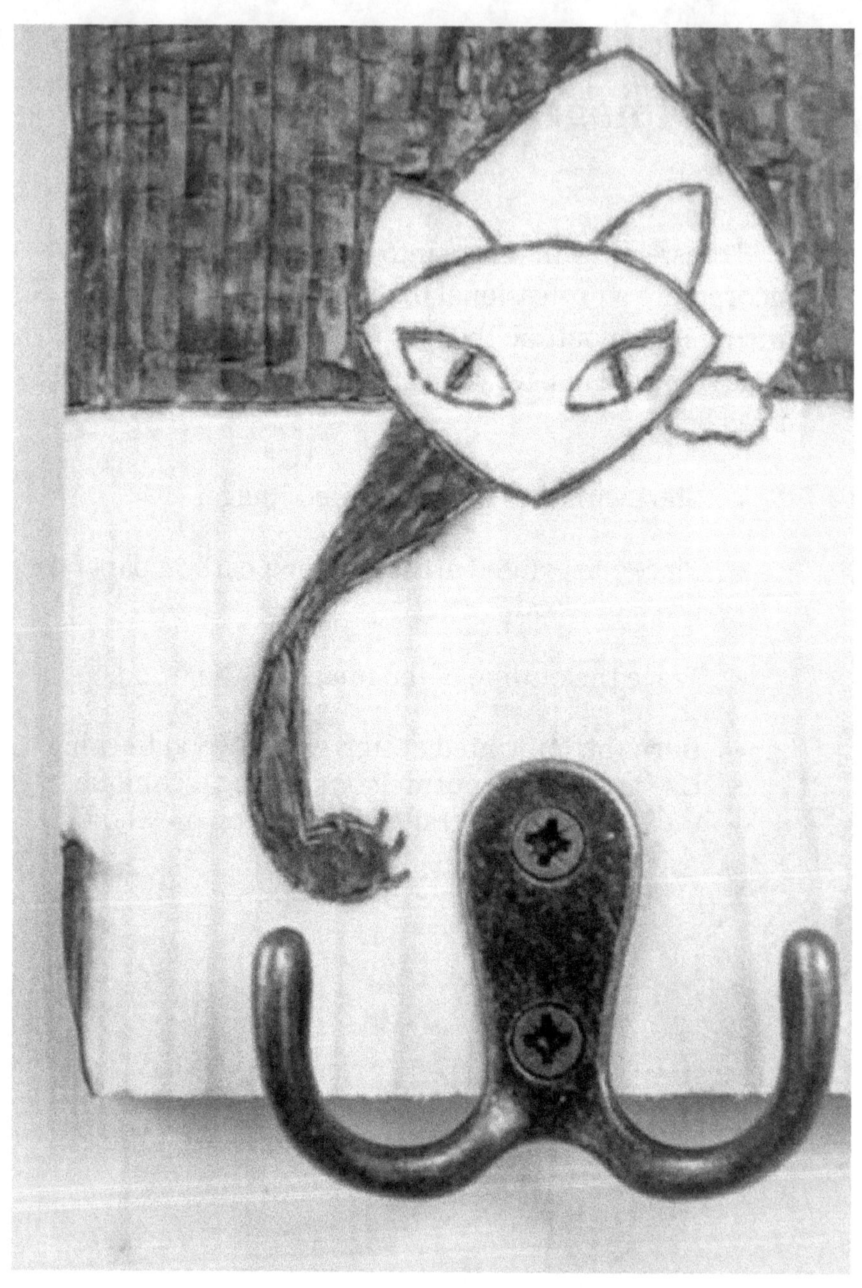

Each of these steps are explained in greater detail below:

- *Print the Desired Image* – Download your desired digital image from the publicly available images approved for use and print it using an inkjet or laser printer. This technique is very useful as you can obtain images that contain a very high level of detail. It helps you successfully create complex pyrography artwork that may not be possible with hand drawn techniques.

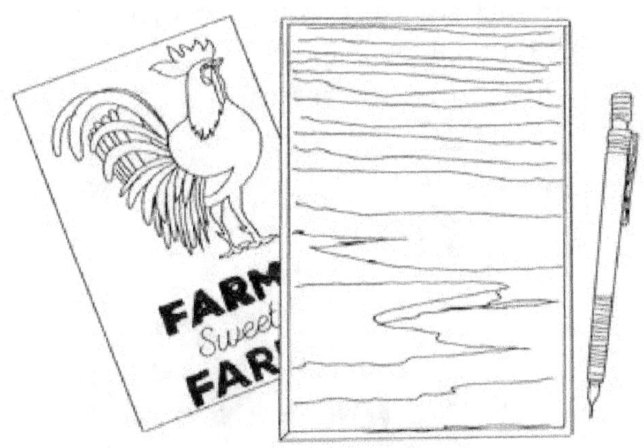

- *Place the Carbon Paper and Printed Image on the Wood* – Carbon paper serves as a good medium to recreate a flawless design on wood. Carbon paper was originally used with a typewriter. Typists would place the carbon paper between two papers while typing the text and obtain the impression on the other paper at the same time. The original text would be the ink from the typewriter, and the text in the other paper would be the blue or black color of the carbon paper.

After you select the desired color of the carbon paper, cut it to an appropriate size and place it securely on wood. You need to make sure the glossy side of the carbon paper is facing the wood. The carbon paper should not move until you complete the transfer. You may want to use masking tape to secure the carbon paper onto your piece of wood. Now place your printed paper at an appropriate position, preferably the center of your wooden block. You may secure the printed paper with masking tape as well to prevent it from moving.

- *Trace the Image Outline on Wood* – Use a sharp pencil or pen tip to trace the outline of the printed image. Use enough pressure so that an outline of the image is printed on the wooden block. You may transfer all or parts of the image, as you intend to achieve the final artwork.

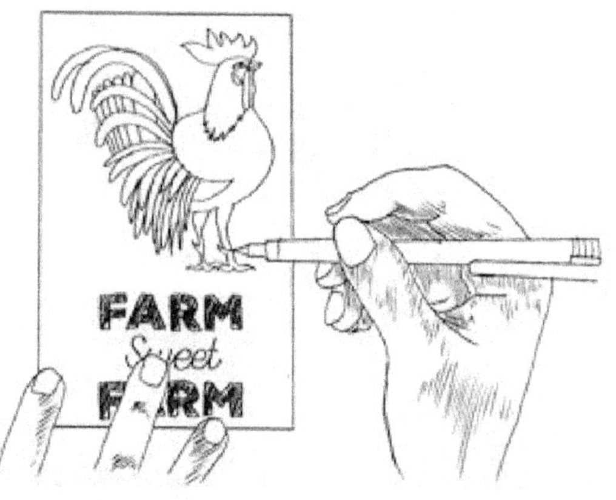

However, it is important to plan beforehand, exactly which parts of the image you want to transfer, as the lines imprinted on wood using carbon paper cannot be erased. The only way to erase the lines, if need be, is to use sandpaper to smooth out the parts that were imprinted on the wood.

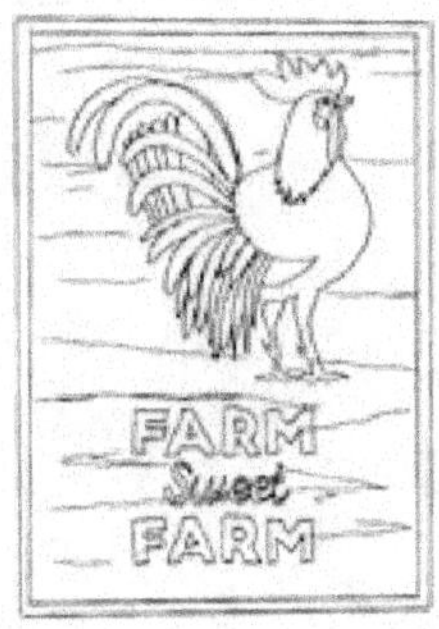

- *Burn the Design Using a Wood Burning Tool* – The final step is to burn the design with the help of a wood burning tool. You may use a solid-point burner or wire-tip burner with a burn tip of your choice to achieve the desired effect for your artwork.

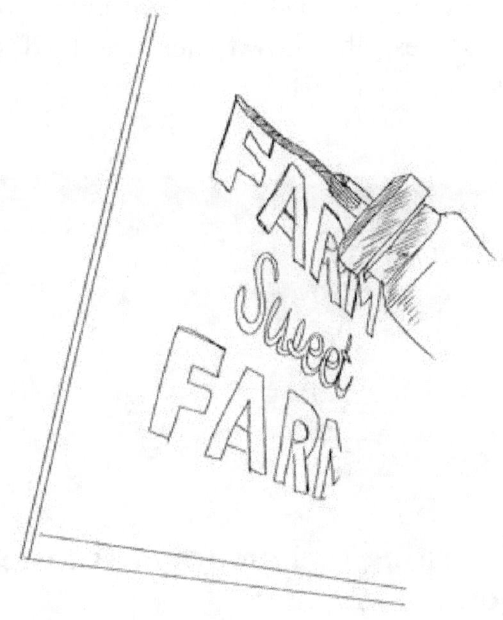

For more information on using the most suitable burning tool and an appropriate nib for your artwork, refer to chapter

3 on using wood burners and the different burn tips available for the purpose.

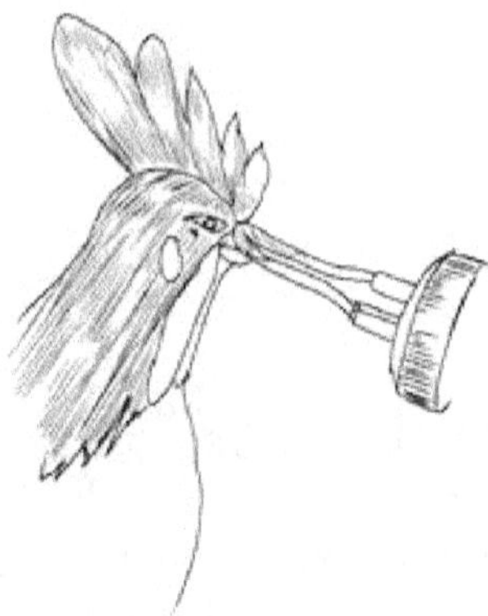

Chapter 5 describes basic line techniques for burning wood and also describes how to achieve the desired shading effect for your piece of art.

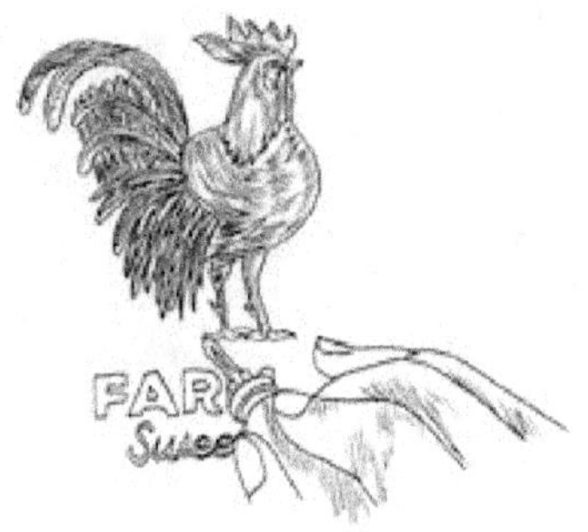

Other Interesting Techniques to Transfer Printed Patterns on Wood

While using carbon paper to transfer your printed artwork on wood is the oldest and easiest technique, there are a number of ways you can transfer the design on wood.

- Tracing and Retracing Using Chalk or Pencil – In this technique, you place the printed pattern face down on wood and trace the image outline with the chalk or pencil. Later, you flip the printed paper so that the chalk or graphite is in contact with the wood. Then you retrace the outline to create an imprint on the wood. When tracing with this technique, you must make sure you do not apply too much pressure so that you do not end up engraving the wood.

- Rubbing the Flip Side of the Printed Pattern – This is the simplest technique, but provides a fragile imprint to work with. You may want to use the technique with drawings that do not have a very high level of detail. To work with the technique, you place the paper face down in your piece of wood and rub the back side of the printed pattern with chalk. This method works best when the digital printout is obtained using an inkjet printer. On rubbing the back of the design, a light outline is produced on your block of wood. This technique gives you an imprint that does not last long and you have to start working with it immediately.

- Use Transfer Paper to Recreate the Digital Pattern on Wood – Transfer paper contains a coating of wax and pigment. It is also known as graphite paper or freezer paper. When using transfer paper, you cut it to the same size as your piece of wood. Once you have the right size of transfer paper, you place it on the wood and then place your printed design on the printed paper. Subsequently, you may trace the printed design with a stylus while applying medium pressure. You must take care not to apply too much pressure, as it may lead to blurred lines. When you are done with the tracing step, carefully take off your printed paper and transfer paper from the piece of wood. This will give you a grey design as opposed to the dark lines obtained from carbon paper. A transfer paper is sometimes more preferable than a carbon paper since it provides a lighter impression. You can easily erase parts of the image, unlike a carbon paper that provides a more permanent design.

Successfully transferring the digitally printed design on wood is the first step to producing professional artwork. Regardless of the transfer technique, it is important to remember that lighter woods allow the design to show up clearly when compared to the darker counterpart. To produce clean artwork, sand the wood surface using a 60-80 grit sandpaper. This will help you obtain a smooth surface. Sanding the surface of the wood also ensures that the ink is absorbed well into the wood surface.

If you are not happy with the transfer, you may correct errors using various techniques such as erasing with a graphite eraser (for transfer paper), using wet sponge (in the case of fragile transfer), or sanding (when using carbon paper). After removing the ink from unwanted parts of the image, you may reassemble the printed image on the surface of the wood and retrace it to obtain the desired image.

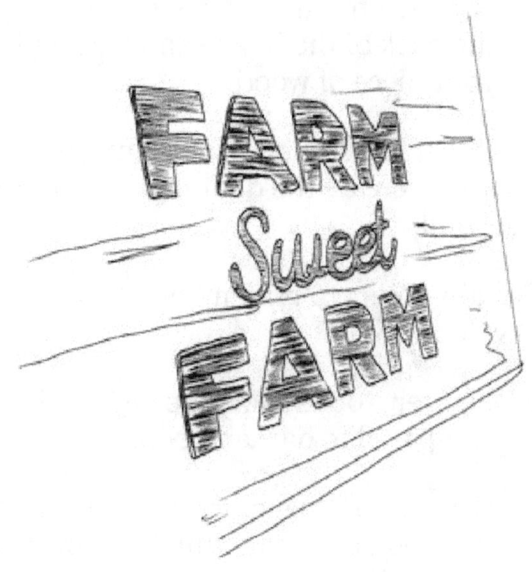

Chapter Summary

- Transferring image to your block of wood is a simple process:

  - Print your selected image and place the printed image on carbon paper over your block of wood.

  - Trace the image outline on wood using the tip of a pen. Trace the whole image or parts of it as you may want to achieve in your final artwork.

  - Use a burn tool to burn the design on wood. Use a suitable burn tip to achieve the desired effect.

- Other techniques may also be used to transfer the image to your piece of wood:

  - Use chalk or pencil to trace the reverse side, and then flip the image and retrace to get an impression on wood.

- o Obtain a fragile imprint of the image by rubbing the back of the image and placing it face down on your piece of wood.

  - o Use transfer paper containing wax and pigment and recreate the digital pattern of the image on wood.

- Certain points to remember when transfering images to wood include:

  - o Lighter woods show the design clearly when compared to darker wood.

  - o Using a sandpaper to create a smooth surface for the wood allows the ink from the carbon paper to be absorbed well.

  - o To correct errors, you may use a wet sponge when the image imprint is light, graphite paper for transfer paper, or sanding in the case of carbon paper.

In the next chapter you will learn how to burn Lichtenberg figures using high voltage discharge.

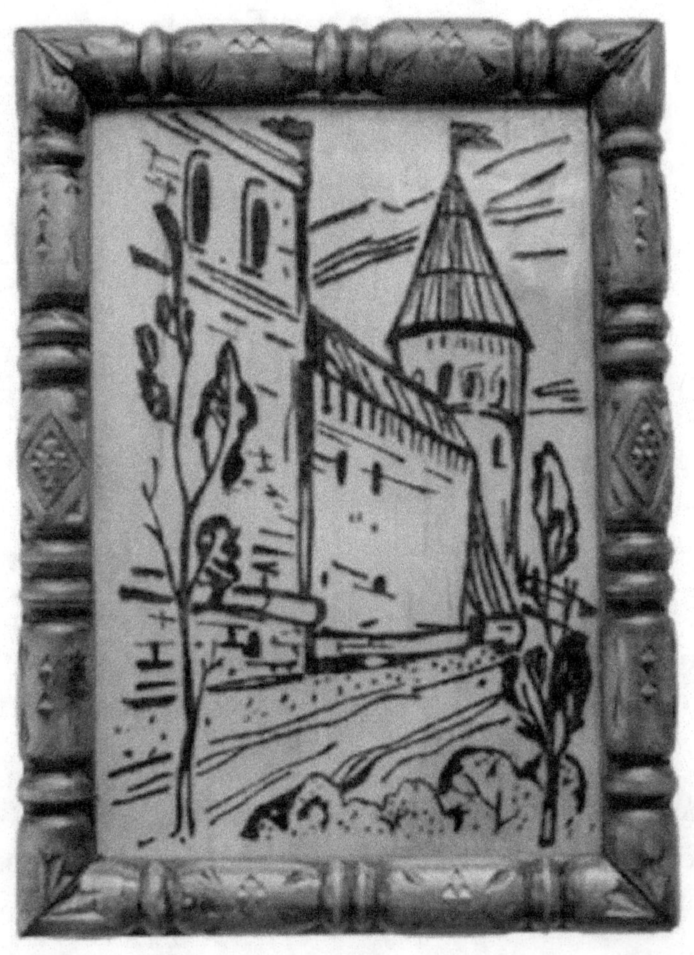

Chapter Eight:
Wood Burning with Lichtenberg Figures - Ampere (High Voltage Discharge)

Creating Lichtenberg figures on wood is a recent development in pyrography. The art is also referred to as fractal wood burning. Tree-like figures are burnt in wood by supplying a high voltage through a transformer. The transformer is potentially dangerous and must be used with caution.

Overview of the Burn Process and Discussion of Important Considerations when Burning Lichtenberg Figures in Wood

Sanding the Wood - An important aspect of burning Lichtenberg figures in wood is to use sandpaper and make the surface of the wood smooth enough to work with. An 800 grit sandpaper usually serves the purpose.

Ionization Solution for Wood Conductivity - Another consideration is about applying a solution with good electrical conductivity on the surface of the wood as dry wood does not conduct electricity. The conducting solution may be applied with a tablespoon of baking soda and a cup of warm water. A thick paint brush works well and any excess solution is soaked up by the wood in about five minutes.

Types of Transformers - It is also important to understand the role of the transformer in creating Lichtenberg figures. High voltage electrical current is applied by the transformer. Pyrographers may use an oil burner transformer, microwave oven transformer, or a neon sign transformer for the purpose. When the high voltage is applied, an electrical current of extremely high intensity is released. The current is transferred into the wood with the help of two probes. Wood burns between two probes in the form of distinctive figures, commonly referred to as Lichtenberg figures.

Lichtenberg figures or fractal burns create images that resemble a lightening. The transformers require 120 volts and produce 2000-15000 volts. Microwave oven transformers (MOT) produce 2000 volts output and their typical rating is 5 amps. The wattage for a microwave transformer that produces 2000 volts is 700 watts. The transformer creates aggressive burns on wood and may become the cause of hazard when not used cautiously. Microwave oven transformers create deep and wide burns. Furthermore, the voltage produced by a neon sign transformer measures between 9000 and 15000 volts. The typical voltage rating of a neon sign transformer is 12000 volts and their amperage is 35 ma. Neon sign transformers burn slowly but create more detailed patterns. However, they have a lower amperage and can create more detailed patterns. Moreover, oil burner transformers have 10000 volts rating and an amperage of 23 ma. They can produce a high level of detail on wood and are safest among the three types of transformers.

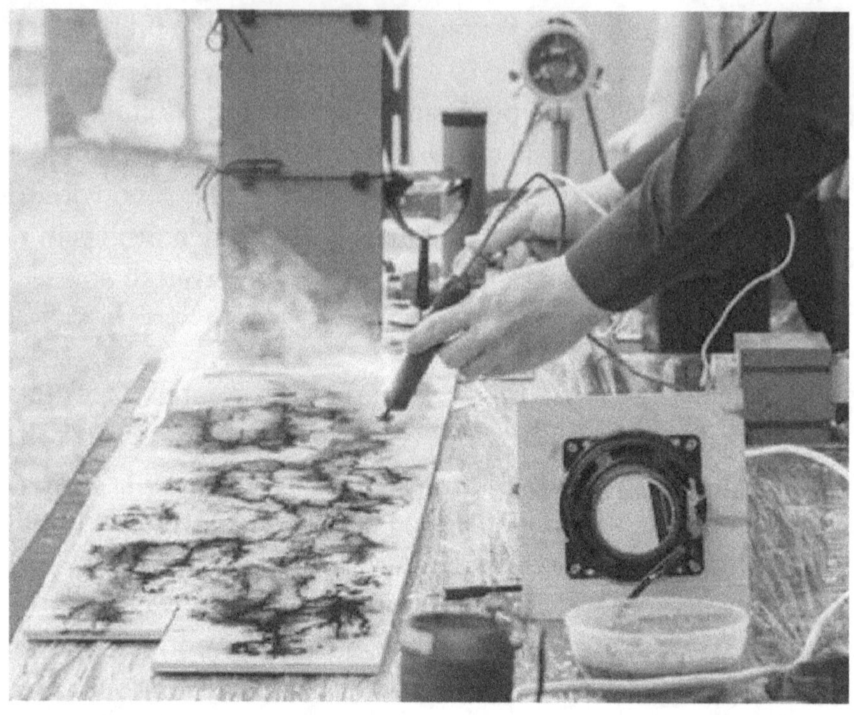

Placement of Probes - Probes may be placed on the wood without touching them so that the Lichtenberg pattern is created between the selected points. Alternatively, the probes may be hand-held to be able to burn the pattern with greater control. When using hands-on probes, all types of insulating material may be used, such as PVC sticks attached to an electrical tape. Alternatively, wooden rods may be used to provide the desired insulation. The electrical cables are attached using various methods such as using a soldering iron, screws, or clamps. Hand-held probes carry a high level of risk as you are in the vicinity of 2000-15000 volts of electricity. In the event of a hazard, it is extremely difficult to switch off the unit unless a Deadman switch is available. Hands-off probes may be more preferable since you don't have to touch the probes or any part of the machine while working with it. The setup of the probe consists of PVC insulation and clamps soldered on the cable with a copper brass rod. Alternatively, the clamps may be soldered on the band with a nail and screw. When using hands-on probes, you have to turn off your machine to move your probes. In most cases, hands-off probes are safest and most effective. Hands-on probes are only effective when working with round pieces of wood since it would be difficult to retain the probe on the surface of the wood.

Burning Effectively - Probes are placed on the surface of the wood and current applied through the probes. The burn figures crawl towards each other to resemble the fine branches of a tree. Different branches may be created in the wood by moving the probe from one point to the next on the surface of the wood. Whenever the wood seems particularly dry due to the application of the current from extremely high voltage, a layer of conductive liquid may be applied to allow the Lichtenberg figures to crawl at a constant speed. A very slow pace makes the figures appear crowded. They may even get a scorched look. If your speed is too fast, the figures will not branch consistently and you may not be able to get the desired appearance.

Further, when your wood does not burn well, it may so happen that the wood is either too dry or too wet. You will be able to get the perfect burn speed when the wood is neither too wet nor too dry. Eventually, practicing the technique leads to best results.

Washing and Finishing up - After burning the Lichtenberg figures, the piece of wood must be cleaned by running water over it. Place the finished piece of wood in a deep sink and allow water to flow over it while scrubbing it to remove the char and reveal the figures. You may continue to scrub the wood until all the char is removed. Allow the wood to dry. To sand the burns, a 400-1000 grit sandpaper is appropriate. You must take care not to sand the figures themselves as you may end up losing the fine details.

Safety Considerations – It is important to note that burning Lichtenberg figures is a dangerous project and requires patience. To perform the experiment successfully while working with high voltage requires the use of insulated gloves. The wood surface must also be insulted and you may involve a friend in your project who can help you with first aid if you succumb to burns from the high voltage. Our previous book on "Beginners Guide to Wood Burning" describes safety measures in detail.

You may also note that working with a transformer carries several risks including the risk of electrocution, leading to lethal shock due to the large quantity of current flowing through it. Further, a significant amount of ultraviolet light is produced from the electrical arc and is harmful to the eyes. It would be a good idea to wear welding goggles or sunglasses to protect your eyes from the harmful radiation. Finally, there is a risk of fires from the large volume of current flowing across the potential difference.

Walkthrough of the Process Used to Create Lichtenberg Figures

A walkthrough of the process of creating Lichtenberg figures is summarized below. To burn your own Lichtenberg figures, you will require the following materials.

Neon Sign Transformer (NST) – As explained in the chapter, a neon sign transformer (NST) uses neon gas, and it's signs are made from tubes filled with gas. High voltage produced by the transformer is supplied to the tube filled with gas. High voltage causes the kinetic energy of the neon atom electrons to increase. This process powers a neon sign. Neon sign transformers generate smaller and lighter designs at a high frequency, and are preferred over iron core transformers.

Alligator Clips – Two alligator clips may be used to secure the probes on your piece of wood and create the Lichtenberg figures.

Piece of Plywood – A 1.5 cm thick piece of plywood serves as a wooden block for your artwork.

Probes – The probes act as end points to create your Lichtenberg figures. You could use either nails coated with copper or brass rods for the purpose.

Insulating Gloves – Insulators minimize risk of shock and are highly recommended.

Baking Soda – You will need baking soda to prepare a solution you may apply on the piece of wood so it can conduct electricity. To make the solution, you will need:

- A tablespoon

- A mixing cup

- 1.5 inch brush

Sandpaper – You will also need 800 grit sandpaper to make the piece of wood smooth. An 800-grit sandpaper works well with most types of wood.

The following steps provide a sequence you may follow to complete the process of burning Lichtenberg figures on wood.

- *Prepare your Working Area* - Ensure you have someone to accompany you when working with your pyrography project. The first step also requires you to prepare the wood using sandpaper. This helps you achieve a smooth surface to work with. It is essential to wear insulated gloves and place the wood on an insulated surface to minimize the risk of hazard. Your insulating gloves must be able to handle 12000 volts, and such a rating is highly recommended. Placing the wood on an insulated surface also ensures that the electricity flows through the wood.

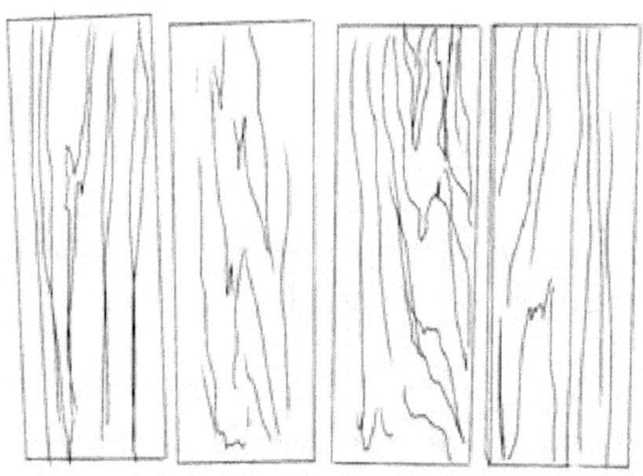

- *Prepare the Ionizing Solution* – Baking soda acts as the key ingredient of your ionizing solution. Add a tablespoon of baking soda to a cup of warm water to make a solution. Apply the solution to the surface of the wood. Allow the wood to soak up the excess solution. When starting your burning project, apply a coat of the solution and wipe off the excess solution from the surface of the wood.

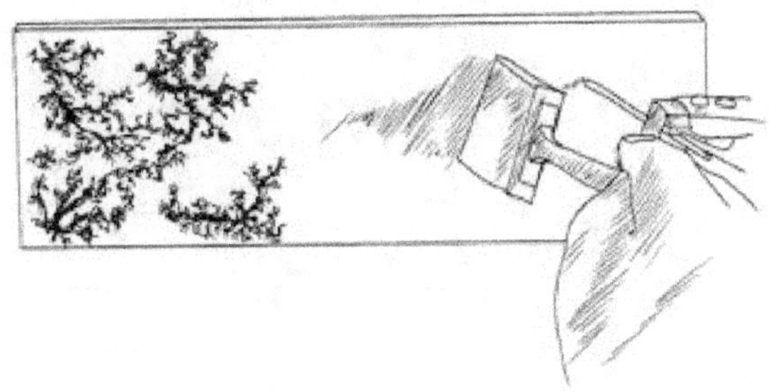

- *Set up the Probes and Alligator Clips* – Your probes must be placed apart with a few inches between them. Turn on your neon sign transformer. You will notice how the figures start crawling towards each other. Use dry wood blocks to hold the alligator clips in place and balance the probes.

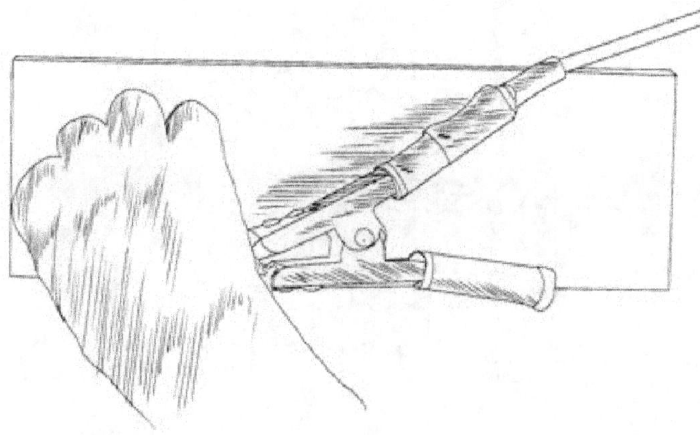

- *Start Burning the Wood* – Once you have the probes and alligator clips in place, it is time to start burning the wood to create beautiful Lichtenberg patterns. You may have to reapply the ionizing solution as the heat from the burning process dries the wood. Maintain the wood at a state that is neither too wet nor too dry. This technique will help you obtain smooth Lichtenberg figures.

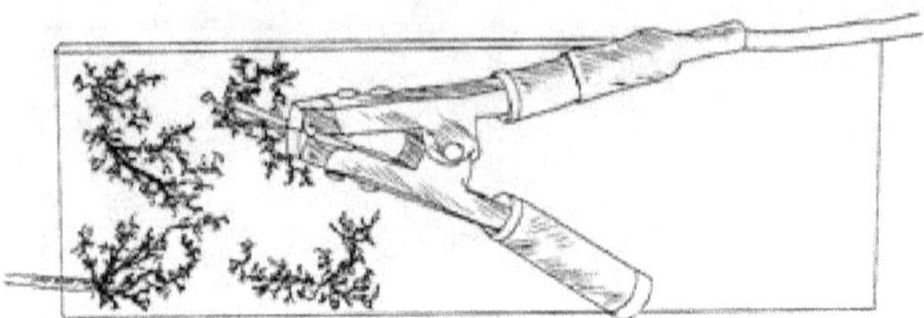

- *Remove the Probes and Clean the Figures* – Once you are satisfied with your design, clean the wood by placing it in a deep sink and running water over it while scrubbing out the charred surface of the wood. A 400-1000 grit sandpaper is ideal for the purpose.

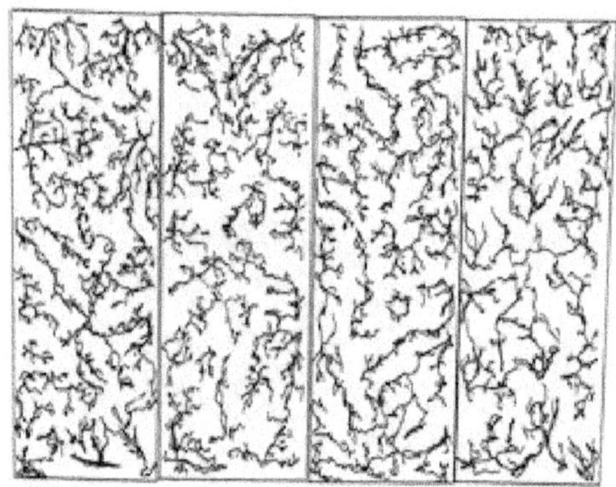

To sum it all up, burning Lichtenberg figures help you beautiful designs in wood without requiring artistic abilities. Overtime, you may gain expertise in achieving distinct artwork as you practice with the different wood burning strokes. In the meantime, it is still possible to successfully produce unmatched artwork with Lichtenberg figures.

Chapter Summary

- Fractal wood burning or Lichtenberg figures is a recent technique in pyrography.

- Lichtenberg figures are created when very high voltage is supplied to the wood with a transformer connected to the leads.

- It is important to understand several aspects of burning Lichtenberg figures:

  - A smooth surface of wood may be achieved by using sandpaper.

  - Apply an ionization solution made from baking soda and warm water for good electrical conductivity.

  - Understand the different types of transformers available (microwave oven transformer, oil burner transformer, and neon sign transformer) and select the right transformer.

  - Use two probes to transfer the current to the wooden block. Probes may be either hands-on probes used with insulating material, or hands-off probes that are left untouched throughout the process.

  - On applying the high voltage, Lichtenberg figures resembling lightening are created on the wood surface

  - To achieve the best results, apply current when the wood is neither too dry nor too wet. Also apply an ionization solution to create consistent branching and avoid scorching the wood.

- o   After finishing up with the burn process, scrub the
    wood under running water and clean it up with
    400-800 grit sandpaper to reveal the Lichtenberg
    figures.

- Follow safety precautions closely as burning
  Lichtenberg figures on wood is a highly dangerous
  process:

  - o   Use insulated gloves when working with high
      voltage.

  - o   Insulate the wood surface.

  - o   Involve a friend who can help with first aid in the
      event of injury.

  - o   Transformers put you at the risk of electrocution
      and lethal shock.

  - o   Working with transformers may cause damage to
      the eyes due to the ultraviolet light emanating
      from the electrical arc. Wear sun glasses or
      welding goggles to protect against the harmful
      radiation

- The Lichtenberg figures project described in this
  chapter follows the steps summarized below:

  - o   Sand the wood with 800-grit sandpaper to achieve
      a smooth surface.

  - o   Prepare a solution of baking soda and apply it on
      the surface of the wood for good electrical
      conductivity.

  - o   A neon sign transformer (NST) is used to generate
      the voltage required to burn Lichtenberg figures.

- Probes may be placed on the wood surface using either brass rods or nails coated with copper. Use alligator clips to secure the probes on the surface of wood.

- Start burning Lichtenberg figures on the wood. Apply the ionization solution periodically to ensure that the surface of wood is neither too wet nor too dry.

- Remove the probes and clean the wood surface with 400-1000 grit sandpaper by placing it in the sink and running water over it.

In the next chapter you will learn how to burn a wood mandala.

Chapter Nine:
How to Wood Burn a Mandala

"Mandala" is a Sanskrit word which means "circle". It consists of a collection of geometric symbols with a spiritual component. Mandalas were originally an integral part of meditation practices in eastern religions such as Jainism, Hinduism, and Buddhism. Contemporary mandalas draw upon certain aspects of ancient spiritual tradition and depict the cosmos. They are symbolic representations of wholeness , connectedness, and healing. Mandalas may be used as a means of self-expression and insight. Experts believe that mandalas may be helpful in relieving stress and anxiety. A mandala is also employed in modern art therapy to promote healing and understand the subconscious mind. Drawing mandalas enhances creativity and may successfully remove emotional blockages. It is an effective means to lessen the trauma associated with post traumatic stress disorder (PTSD). Children with attention deficit hyperactivity disorder (ADHD), or those exhibiting impulsive behavior may also benefit from mandalas. Since mandalas are regarded as symbolic representations of the Universe, they are sometimes perceived as tools to enhance self-discovery.

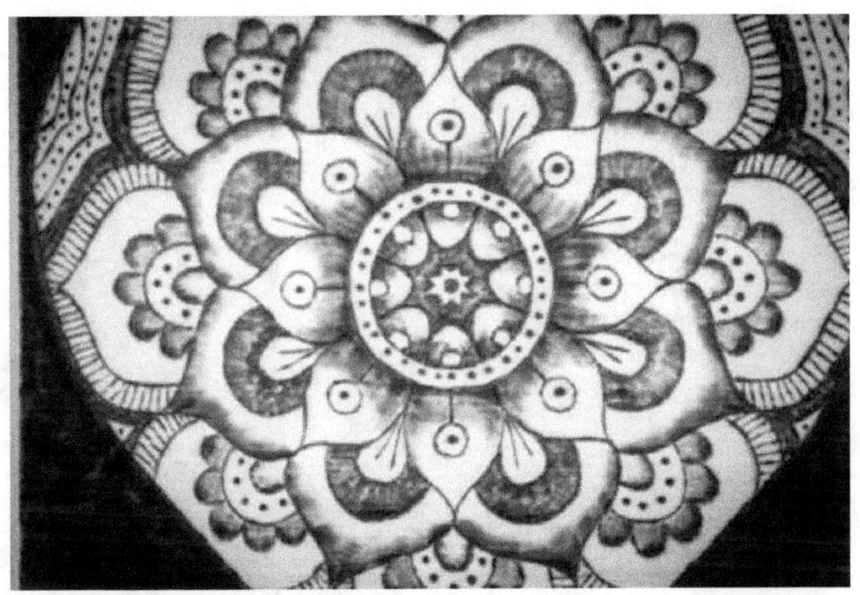

A basic mandala consists of a square with four gates that have a circle with a center point. Radial balance is an intrinsic feature of mandalas.

Creating mandalas on wood is the culmination of two relaxing techniques and produces attractive artwork. Mandala pyrography acts as a stress reliever and has a soothing effect on the eyes. To create a mandala on wood, you will need:

- A piece of wood

- 400-grit sandpaper

- Stencil

- Heat-sensitive marker

- Blow torch with propane

- Epoxy

- Thick tape

- Detail torch with butane

The process of wood burning a mandala is described below.

- Obtain a smooth wood surface using sandpaper. As mentioned before, a 400-1000 grit sandpaper may serve the purpose. Wipe off the surface of the wood

using a clean cloth. You could also use a variety of
other materials to sand the wood and achieve a
smooth surface. For example, you may use a sanding
sponge and tack cloth or cheesecloth for cleaning the
wood.

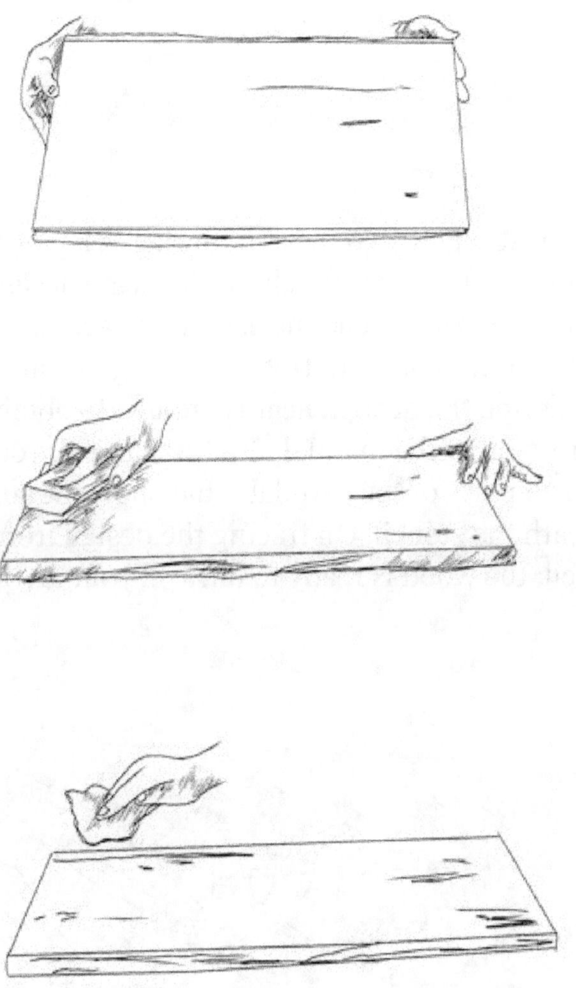

- Now place the stencil at an appropriate position on
  the wood surface, and use a masking tape or thick

tape to hold it securely in place. Trace the design of the mandala using a heat-sensitive marker.

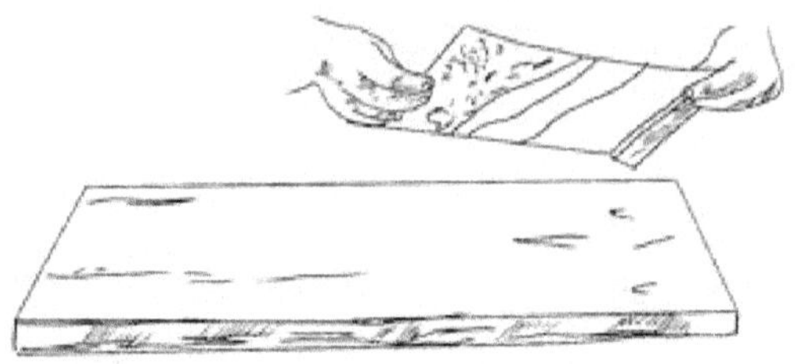

A heat sensitive or scorch marker is a fine-tip wood burning tool that helps achieve intricate designs on wood. It contains non-toxic chemicals that are activated by heat. The marker may be used to trace the design from the stencil. On completing the design, heat is applied to obtain the impression of the mandala. In this project, you may want to trace all parts of the mandala that show the surface of wood beneath the stencil. On tracing the design from the mandala stencil, the wood is ready to unravel your artwork.

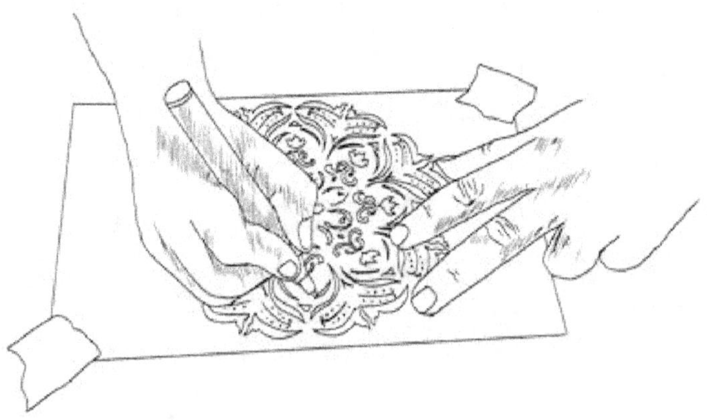

- Your next step is to burn the wood. In this case, a propane blow torch is used to reveal the design in wood. The wood plank is placed on a few pieces of wood over concrete or stone floor. The wood is torched slowly from one end to another. Applying the heat causes the pattern to appear due to the chemicals in the scorch pen. Then the butane torch is applied to achieve greater precision.

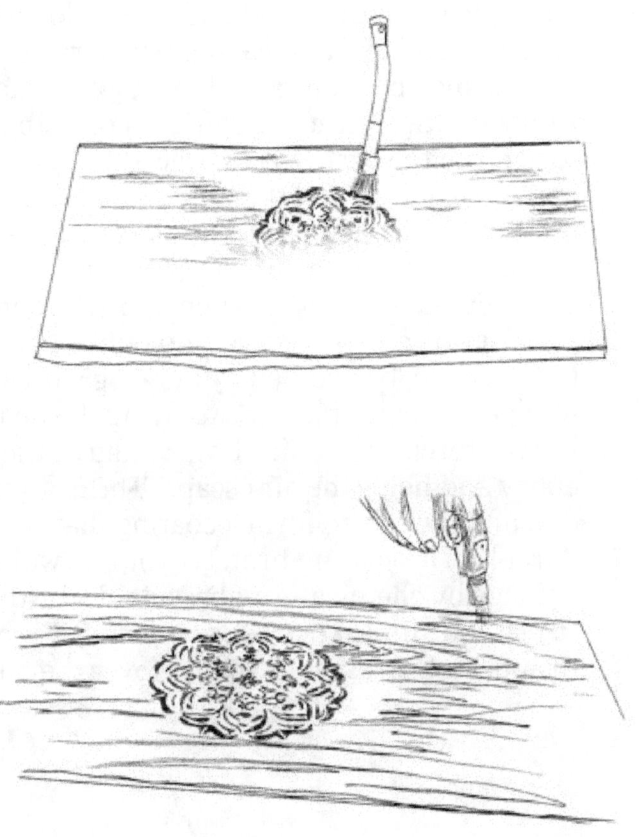

- On finishing with the blow torches, the next step is to coat the surface with epoxy. Epoxy is essentially a polymer with resistance and mechanical properties. Epoxy coatings consist of a resin and hardener. The epoxy coating is prepared by combining the resin and hardener. The resin and hardener is mixed in a specific ratio such as 1:1 or 2:1, as indicated by the manufacturer. A chemical reaction occurs as the two constituents are combined.

- The final step is to apply the epoxy to the wood surface. Epoxy creates a clean coating on wood to enhance the wood and grain. It provides four times the thickness of polyurethane. Before applying the epoxy, verify if the wood has cooled down to achieve an even coating. An ideal temperature of 18 degrees Celsius may be maintained throughout the process. Apply multiple thin coats instead of a single thick coat to achieve the best results. Use a sponge roller to apply the epoxy, and then drag another roller to tip off. Multiple coats may be applied progressively, checking to see if the previous coat is tacky prior to applying the next coat. When applying epoxy to the wood, ensure that there are no bubbles trapped. Air bubbles may be avoided by blowing with a butane torch or a hot air blower. Applying the heat with a butane torch or hot air blower reduces the viscosity of epoxy and helps the air escape. The coating is left to dry, and it cures to form a coating that is rigid and durable. The coating protects your artwork from damage by chemicals or abrasion. In case you choose to use your finished artwork outside, it is a good idea to apply a UV resistant coating over the epoxy coat.

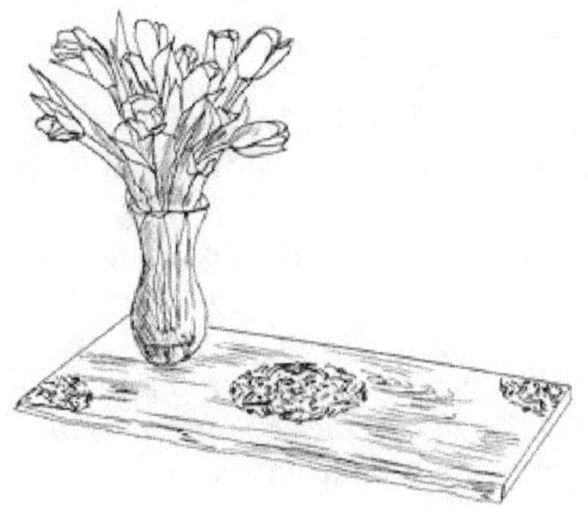

Notes about mixing epoxy resin and hardener:

- Always verify whether the resin and hardener is compatible. Constituents that are manufactured by the same company usually match up perfectly and combine well.

- When determining quantities to be mixed, it is recommended you combine the quantities by volume rather than by their weight. Determining the quantities by weight may be misleading as the constituents may have different densities. When using volume to combine the two components, you may use a cup to measure the resin. Pour the resin into the cup and wait for it to level out. Later, add the exact same volume of the second component.

- When mixing the resin and hardener, it is important to record the ambient temperature. When the ambient temperature is below 20 degrees Celsius, the resin cures very slowly. Slow curing also produces a wax-like layer over the surface that must be removed. A significant drop in the temperature below 20 degrees Celsius causes the epoxy to crystallize. Temperatures above 20 degrees Celsius increase the reaction time of the resin.

- Also note that the hardener also reacts with air, especially if the humidity content is above 65%.

- A tool with straight sides is most effective when mixing the resin and hardener so that any material that sticks to the sides and bottom of the container may be thoroughly stirred and combined. A spatula may be a good choice of tool to mix equal quantities of the resin and hardener.

- Abstain from adding water to the resin as you may not get the required consistency for the final product.

- Finally, use a large container to combine the resin and hardener well.

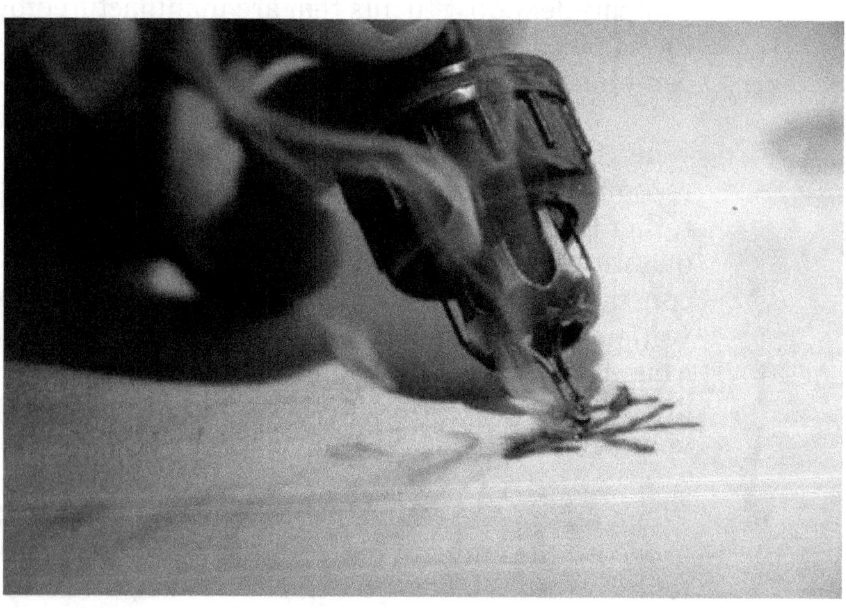

Chapter Summary

- Mandalas consist of geometric symbols arranged in a circle

- They form a part of meditation practices in eastern religions

- They may be effective in treating several conditions such as posttraumatic stress disorder (PTSD) and attention deficit hyperactivity disorder (ADHD).

- Mandalas may be created by wood burning using a simple process:

- Use 400-1000 grit sandpaper to obtain a smooth wood surface and wipe it clean with a soft cloth.

- Place the mandala stencil on the wood surface and secure it with masking tape.

- Trace the design of the mandala using a heat-sensitive marker.

- Use a propane blowtorch to burn the wood and reveal the mandala design imprinted in the previous step.

- Coat the wood surface with epoxy by preparing a mixture of its resin and hardener.

- Adhere to guidelines on mixing the resin and hardener of the epoxy (calculating volume, recording ambient temperature, noting humidity content, using the right mixing tool, combining the constituents in a large container, and abstaining from adding water to the final product).

In the next chapter you will learn how to make a special Christmas Box using the wood burning skills you learned so far.

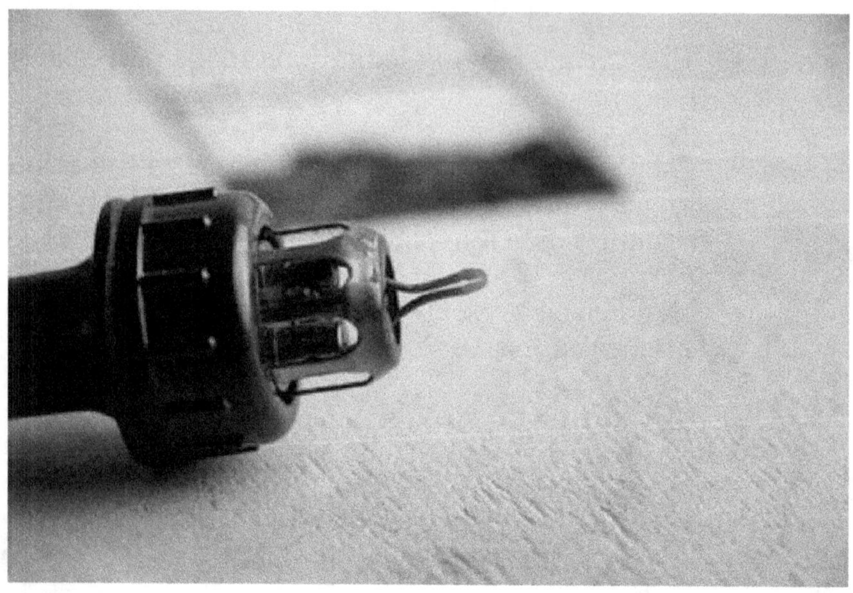

Chapter Ten:
Special Project - Making a Christmas Box with Wood Burning

This chapter describes how you can make a Christmas Box using your wood burning skills. To make a customized Christmas Box using your pyrography skills, you will need the following materials.

- A wooden box of your choice

- A wood burning tool

- 800-grit sandpaper

- Tracing paper

- Crafter's toolset (round head)

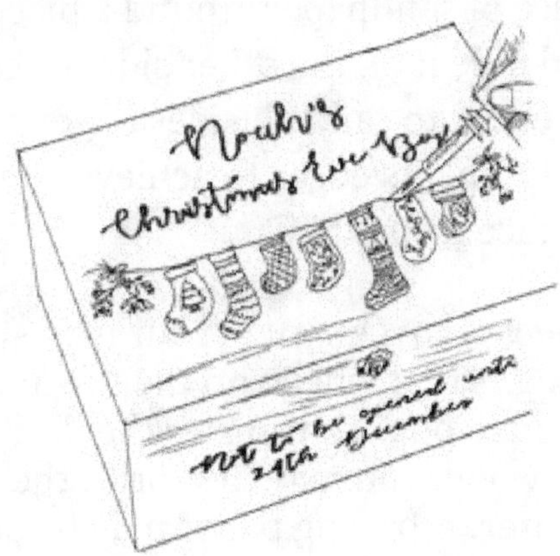

You will use your skills related to burning lines and curves on wood as well as shading skills, to complete your

Christmas project. The following steps guide you through a simple process of preparing a Christmas Box.

- *Sanding the Christmas Box* – Your first step is to use sandpaper to prepare your Christmas Box. An 800 grit sandpaper works best to achieve a smooth surface. Sanding will remove any traces of paint or stain on the surface. It provides a clean and smooth surface.

  Sanding may be done using different grades of sandpaper – from coarsest to finest. Start with the coarse grade sandpaper and follow it up with one of the finer grades of sandpaper. Remove the dust from sanding and also remove any buildup on the sandpaper itself for the best results. Rub the sandpaper on the surface of the wood in a back and forth motion for the best results.

  A sanding block is also a popular way to sand down the surfaces. To make your own sanding block, wrap a piece of sandpaper around a piece of foam or wood, and tape it on the other side to secure it in place. It is essential to sand all sides of your wooden box including its edges to achieve a uniform and smooth surface throughout.

- *Select your Design* – Your next step is to select the designs that will go on the top and/sides of your wooden box. To transfer the design to the surface of the wood, you may first print them with a laser printer. A tracing paper may be used to print these figures so you can transfer then to the wood easily.

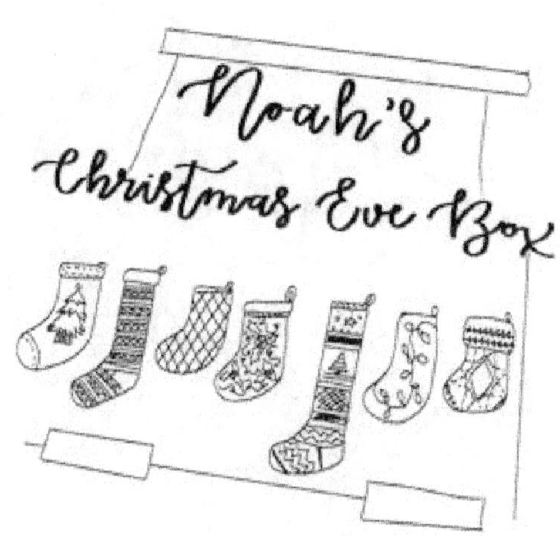

- *Transfer the Design to the Wood* – Once you have the design(s) on tracing paper, place the printed tracing paper where you would like to transfer the design on wood. Use the round-headed crafting tool to trace the edges of the design and leave an imprint of your chosen design on the wooden box.

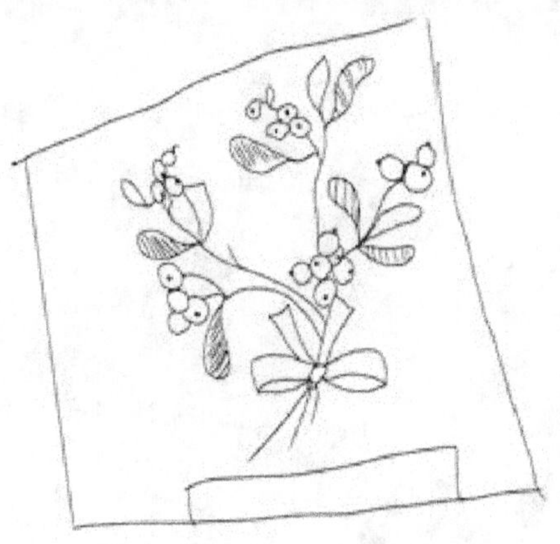

- *Highlight the Design* – Use a marker to highlight the design for wood burning.

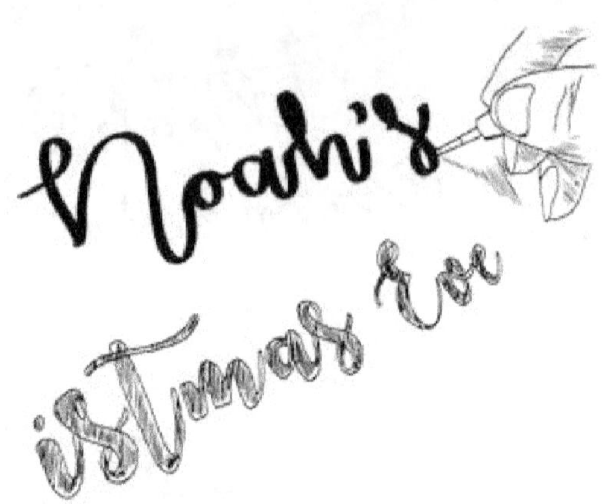

- *Burn the Wood* – Your box is now ready for wood burning. Use your preferred wood burning tool and burn tip to create the edges of your artwork. Create lines and curves according to the basic lines technique for wood burning. This topic is covered in Chapter five. Use the tip of the burn tool or whole edge according to the details in the design. You may even use curves and meandering lines to create curves in your Christmas Box design.

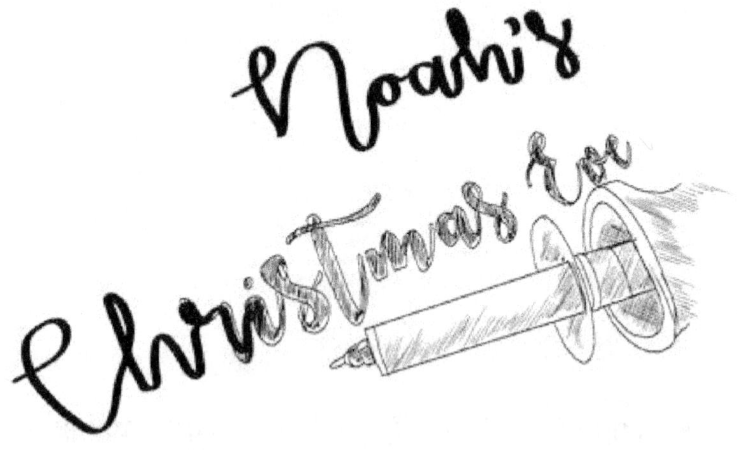

- *Shade the Required Parts of the Image* – Your next step is to fill areas with a shading technique. Vary pressure and apply the right shading effect inside the borders you created with the wood burning tool. As explained in Chapter five, apply less pressure on medium heat for lighter shades, and more pressure for darker shades on wood. Also recollect the different methods of shading discussed in the chapter.

  The desired shading may be achieved by applying an appropriate degree of heat. The amount of heat you apply determines the level of contrast and opacity. Also note that repeated circular movements achieved using gentle pressure on medium heat darken a pecific area. Gradients are achieved by moving from a lower to higher heat setting. Finally, exercise caution when you encounter grain in wood as it may be challenging to achieve the desired shading in those areas. It is best to work with gentle pressure and increase the level of heat gradually to shade the region containing the grain in wood.

  Further, several shading techniques are available to choose from, such as hatching, cross-hatching, creating textures, and backgrounds.

  Common shading techniques are reiterated below to provide a brief about the best effects you can achieve for your Christmas Box.

  o   A smooth fill may be achieved with circular movements on medium heat.

  o   Gradients are achieved with flat tips on medium heat, although the heat setting may have to be calibrated whenever required.

o When gradients are not your preferred methods of filling areas, you may use hatching and cross-hatching even when the wood contains grain. Hatching is achieved by drawing in one direction to achieve parallel strokes, followed by cross-hatching in the perpendicular direction to achieve the desired effect.

o You may settle for a texture and fill a particular area, depending on the nature of your design. For hair-like textures, use the flat tip on high heat. Furry textures are achieved by varying heat to depict darker and lighter areas. Leathery textures may be achieved by making dark edges. Textures are described in greater detail at the end of Chapter five entitled "Basic Line Techniques for Wood Burning".

- *Use Sandpaper to Smoothen your Artwork* – Use a sandpaper, preferably higher grit sandpaper, to finely erase any unwanted burn stains on the clear surface. The sandpaper may also be used to smooth out any rough edges that have formed after the wood burning. After using fine grit sandpaper to clean up imperfections in the wood, the surface may be wiped clean with a lint cloth or glass cleaning cloth.

- *Use the Desired Wood Finish* – The last step is to use the right wood finish to complete your project. Your Christmas pyrography art may be sealed using a variety of wood finishes. Some common wood finishes include paste wax, danish oil, and polyurethane. An appropriate wood finish protects your wood against dust, moisture, oil, and light.

The wood finish may be applied with a brush, or the wood finish may be sprayed directly on the wood surface. When using a brush to apply the wood finish, use strong, consistent strokes to obtain a uniform coat over the wood surface. Obtaining a good protection for the wood surface is possible with multiple coats of the sealant or wood finish. After finishing the application, allow the wood to dry for 24 hours in order to obtain a protective and durable layer.

Some common wood finishes are described below.

- o *Polyurethane* - Polyurethane is either available as a spray, or it may be brushed onto the surface of the wood to create a matte, semi-matte, or glossy look. Polyurethane incorporates durability in your art and may be applied easily. Oil-based polyurethane provides the best results.

- o *Paste wax* – Paste wax is a natural agent and provides a glossy shine and vibrant look to the wood surface. However, paste wax is not resistant to heat or moisture and does not protect your artwork from scratches or abrasions. Paste wax may serve the purpose only for a short duration.

- o *Oil Finishes* – Oil finishes such as linseed oil may also be used to seal your pyrography artwork. Oil finishes also highlight the grain in wood and can be applied easily. They are resistant to heat and provide a durable finish. An oil finish protects the wood artwork from moisture, which means that there is a lower chance of the wood cracking up. However, your pyrography artwork may still be vulnerable to scratches or weathering even when a coat of oil finish is applied.

- o *UV Inhibitors* – Wood burning projects may be protected from weathering as a result of sun exposure by applying a coat of UV inhibitor to your artwork. The most common UV inhibitor is spar urethane, which is most suitable for pyrography artwork displayed outdoors.

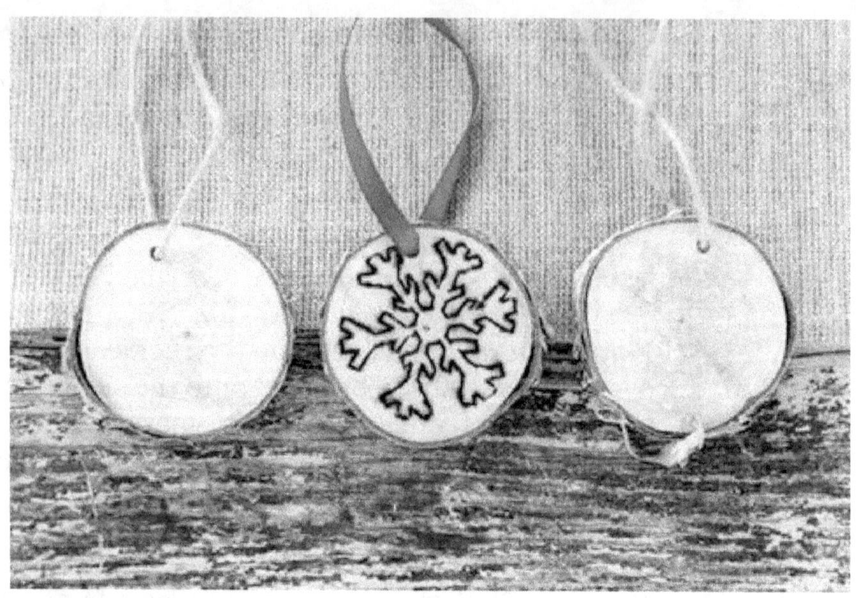

Chapter Summary

- To create a special Christmas Box, you will need the box, a wood burning tool, 800-grit sandpaper, tracing paper, and crafter's toolset

- The steps involved in making your Christmas Box are:

  o Sand the box using an 800-grit sandpaper, followed by finer grades to achieve the right level of smoothness. Either sand directly with the sandpaper or use a sanding block for the purpose.

  o Select the design for the top and sides of the box. Print it with a laser printer on a tracing paper.

  o Transfer the design on the wood surface by tracing its edges using the round-headed crafting tool.

  o Use a marker to highlight the design on wood.

  o Burn the wood using a suitable wood burning tool and burn tip:

- Create the right lines and curve and shade the image using the appropriate intensity of heat.

- Use medium pressure and achieve contrast and opacity by varying the heat setting.

- Use repeated circular movements with gentle pressure to darken an area.

- Apply hatching, cross-hatching, textures, and backgrounds wherever necessary.

- Finish your artwork using sandpaper to erase unwanted stains and smoothen rough edges.

- Use polyurethane, paste wax, or danish oil to create a wood finish.

In the next chapter you will learn how to make attractive fridge magnets.

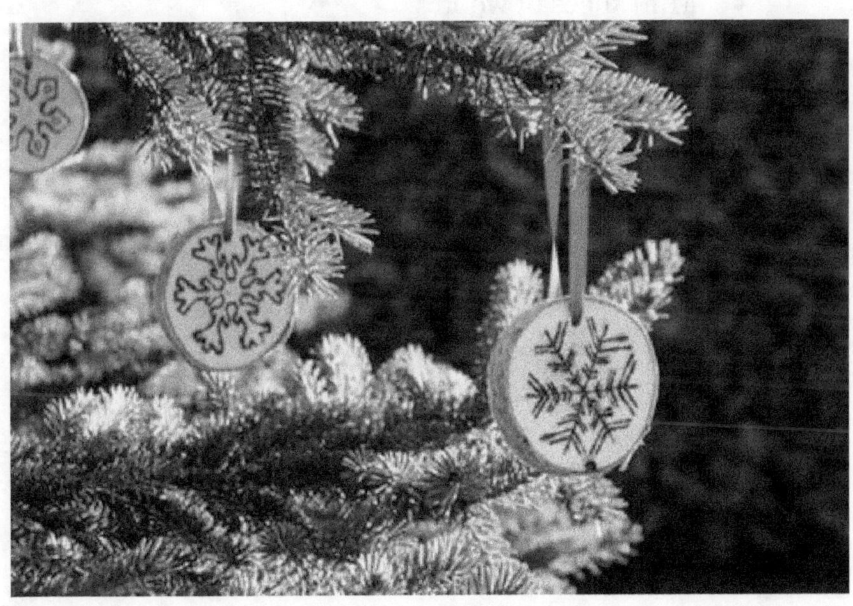

Chapter Eleven:
How to Make Attractive Fridge Magnets

Fridge magnets fascinate children and adults alike. Making do-it-yourself magnets fuels creativity and is a satisfying pursuit. Pyrography for fridge magnets is the best way to create beautiful gifts for special occasions. You can create many different designs and motifs for fridge magnets by wood burning.

The following DIY project takes you through a process of making attractive fridge magnets. To accomplish the project, you need the following materials:

- Mini slices of wood

- Mini magnets

- Wood burning tool

- Glue

- Coloring pen

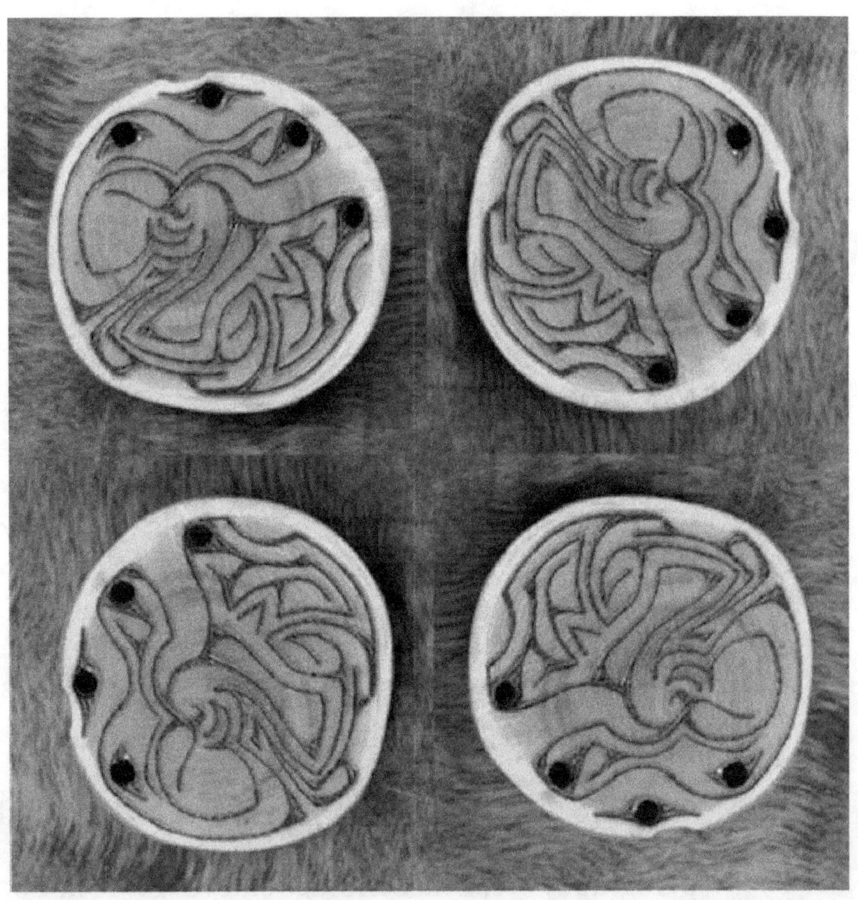

The process of making fridge magnets is described below.

- *Choose a Design for your Wood Slices* – Wood slices are available in different sizes at most craft stores. They may be useful to create a variety of projects including centerpieces, wreaths, seasonal banners, mirror and photo frames. Small wood slices may be used for a variety of craft projects including hooks, fridge magnets, and coasters. As a rule of thumb, you are likely to obtain the best results with natural wood that has not been treated with chemical agents.

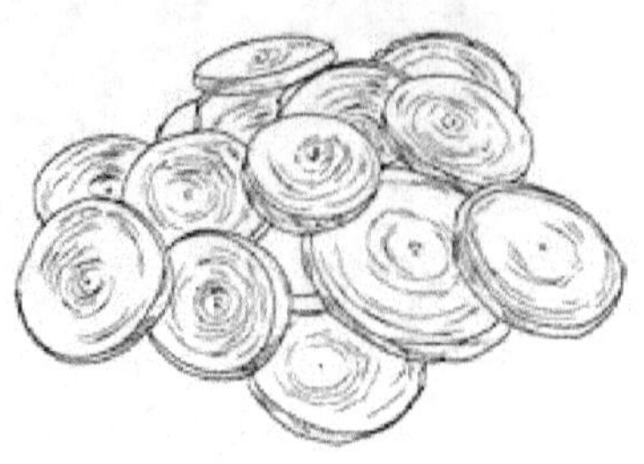

Most pyrographers prefer soft baswood. You may also choose to create your wood burning crafts using pyrography blanks available online. Cut and sanded wooden disks, custom shapes, and disks with round edges are available to create your favorite pyrography artwork. Some examples of wood surfaces for pyrography are baswood country planks, baswood rounds, birch rounds, baswood surfaces, pine, baltic birch plywood, and walnut hollow wood surfaces.

- *Sand the Wood* – The next step is to sand the wood. Sanding is an essential step for professional pyrography artwork. Sanding removes flaws in wood including dents or grooves. A coarse-grit sandpaper may be used to remove scratches. A coarse sandpaper is followed by a fine-grit sandpaper to achieve the required smoothness. You may choose the level of coarseness or fineness of sandpaper (it's grit) after looking at the texture of the wood blank. For example, if you have a wooden block that has been cut using dull knives, you will most likely require sandpaper with coarse grit. On the contrary, if your pyrography blank is made from MDF or plywood, then the wood is usually pre-sanded, and you will require a sandpaper that is less coarse. Furthermore, the technique used for sanding differs from person-to-person. People use different levels of pressure to do the sanding, and may choose a level of coarseness that matches their sanding style. They may also spend varying lengths of time to achieve the required smoothness. A typical approach would be to start with a #80 grit sandpaper, and progress by increasing the level of fineness, from #100, #120, #150, and so on, until the required level of smoothness is achieved. The finest grit chosen is the #180 grit sandpaper and provides the right finish. As mentioned in the previous chapters, it is recommended to sand in the direction of the grain of the wood. Further, you may use a number of methods for sanding including rubbing with sandpaper, rubbing with a sanding block, or using a vibration sander.

- *Transfer Images for Wood Burning* – Once you have the wood surfaces ready, the next step is to transfer the intended images to the wood slices. You may use one of the techniques discussed in the previous chapters, such as using carbon paper or transfer paper. For detailed information, refer Chapter seven on "Image Transfer Techniques". The oldest and easiest technique to transfer a printed image on wood is the carbon paper technique. You may start creating imprints on wood for your fridge magnets by printing the digital motifs using an inkjet or laser printer, and then securely placing the carbon paper on wood, followed by the printed image. You could trace the digital image using a pen to get the carbon paper impression on wood. By the end of this step, you will have wooden disks with the image outlines ready for wood burning.

- *Burn your Artwork and Use Coloring Pencils to Make it More Attractive* – This step requires you to burn your artwork on wood. You can add color to your artwork using colored pens or pencils. You may also use watercolor pencils, oil paints, and dyes to add color to pyrography. These colors are transparent and do not mask the burnt wood color. Instead, they add the right tinge to your pyrography project. We will use colored pencils for our project. These color pencils are generally used by artists and have a wax-based pencil core. Color pencils allow you to create multiple layers of color to achieve the desired hue. Color pencils create a transparent effect even when using multiple layers of color, so that the burnt wood is visible underneath. To achieve the best effect with your color pencils, keep them sharp to get the best results even with grains in wood. You may apply light pressure when coloring your pyrography project. Watercolor pencils also create an interesting effect, and it is possible to spread it using a damp cloth. It is important to note that water-based paints are not always suitable as they may raise the grain in wood. You could also use acrylic paints, crayons, chalk, or pastels to achieve different effects.

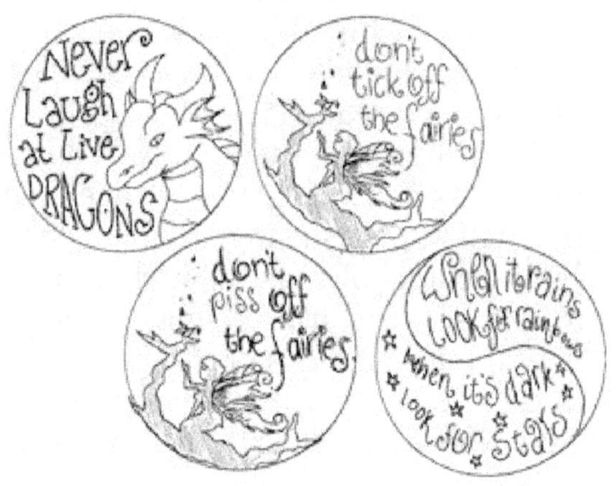

- *Attach Magnets to your Pyrography Art* – Your next step is to attach Magnets to your pyrography artwork with glue. Most pyrographers prefer to work with a hot-melt glue gun. Glue guns offer several advantages including comfortable grip, lightweight, and choice of different angles for effective use. A glue gun warms up in a few minutes, and glue sticks are easily available at most stores. However, glue sticks differ in terms of quality.

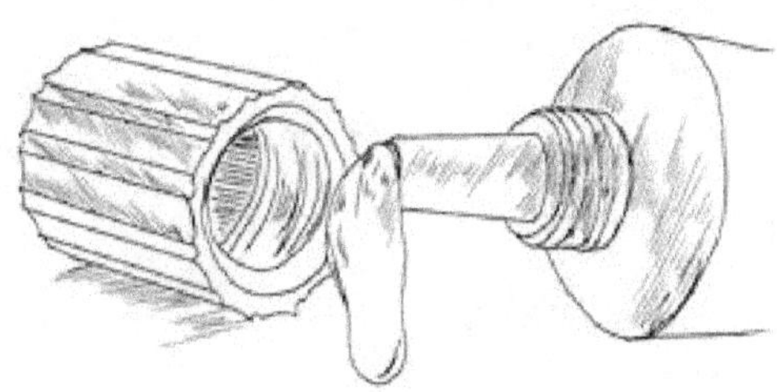

Several factors determine the quality of glue sticks such as resistance to high temperature, performance, and consistency of glue. Further, the most important characteristic of glue used in the hot glue gun is the nature of the bond. You may also evaluate if the glue stick is water-resistant, resistant to impact, and has an extended drying time. It is recommended you choose a glue stick that works at high temperatures as it generally offers a good bonding capability and high performance. For your wood burning project, you may want to apply a blob of high-performance glue and attach the magnet. Hold the magnet in place to fix it securely onto your pyrography magnet.

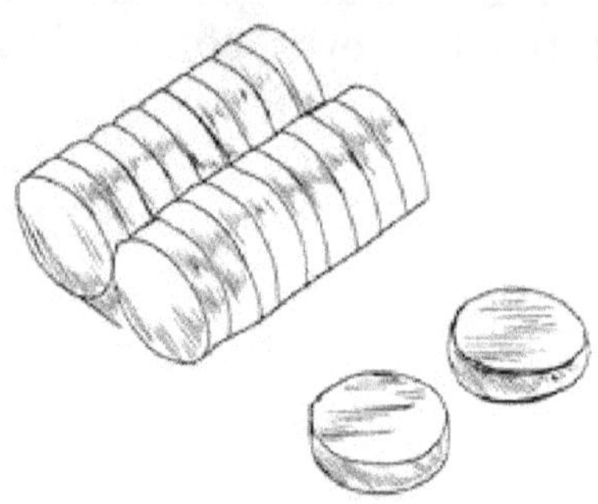

- *Apply the Desired Wood Finish* – Your final step is to apply the desired wood finish to your pyrography project. You may choose from a wide variety of wood finishes including polyurethane, oil finish, paste wax, and optionally, a UV inhibitor. Detailed information on the different types of wood finishes is available in Chapter ten entitled "Special Project – Making a Christmas Box with Wood Burning". Allow your fridge magnets to dry, and your artwork is now ready for display.

The instructions covered in this chapter only touch upon the basics of designing fridge magnets. You can apply the same skills to achieve different types of fridge magnets using pyrography. Some examples include alphabet magnets, number magnets, magnets with symbols, magnets depicting popular sayings, and several other themes (seasons, transport, countries, vegetables, fruits, kitchen items, computer game characters, plants, and colored shapes). Regardless of the theme you choose, fridge magnets impart a pleasing and aesthetic look to your fridge and living area.

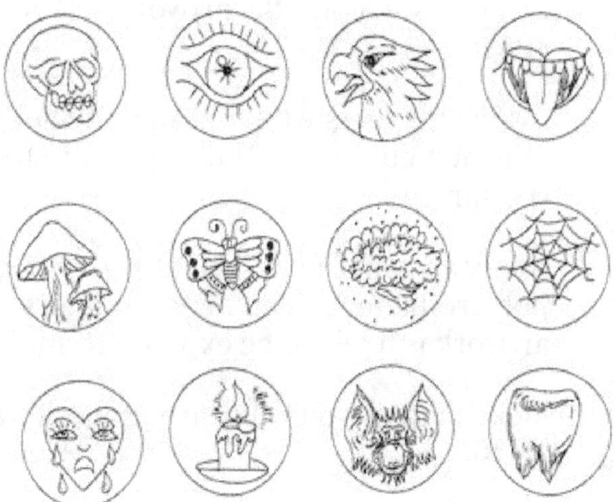

Chapter Summary

- Pyrography may be used to make creative fridge magnets.

- To make fridge magnets, you will need mini wood slices, mini magnets, a wood burning tool, coloring pen, and glue.

- The steps involved in making fridge magnets are included below:

  - Choose a design and select the appropriate wood slices to proceed with your project.

  - Sand the wood to remove imperfections using coarse-grit sandpaper followed by a fine-grit sandpaper.

  - Transfer the printed image to the wood slice using carbon paper or any of the image transfer techniques.

- Use color pencils or crayons, pastels, acrylic paints, and chalk to color the artwork and achieve different effects.

- Attach magnets with high-quality hot glue using a hot-melt gun. Allow the magnets to fix securely to the surface.

- Apply a wood finish such as paste wax or polyurethane, and add UV inhibitors if your artwork is likely to be exposed to sunlight.

In the next chapter you will learn more tips and tricks on shading and line art.

Chapter Twelve:
More Tips and Tricks on Shading and Line Art

Shading is an integral aspect of pyrography as it adds depth to your drawing and helps you achieve different tones of darkness. There are many ways to add life to pyrography projects using the different shading techniques. Shading techniques provide flexibility in creating a wide variety of pyrography artwork such as 3D art.

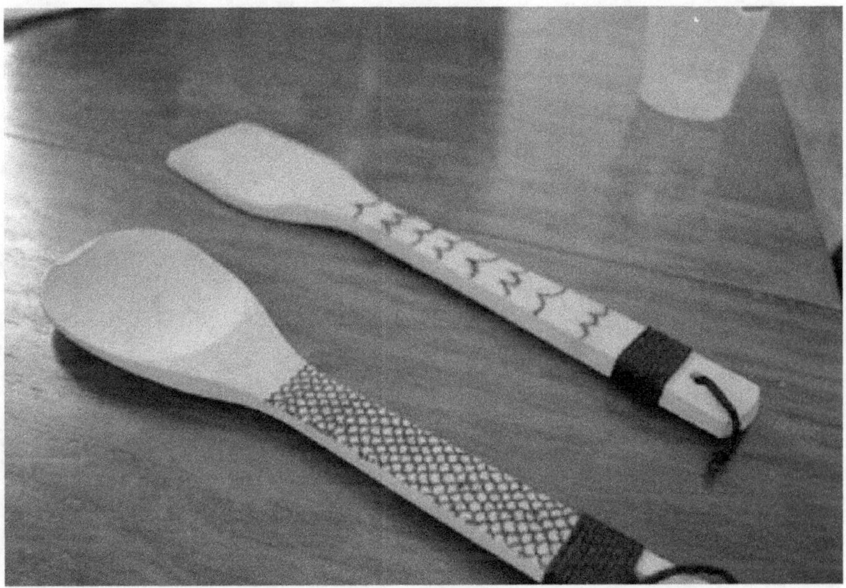

To understand the different aspects of shading by burning wood, try observing a black and white picture to understand the dark and light areas in the image. Learning pencil sketching in another effective approach to identifying strategies for shading in pyrography. The principles applied to pencil shading may be directly applied to your pyrography artwork for smooth transitions between light and dark regions. If you have ever tried sketching before, then you may already be familiar with the effects achieved from varying dark and light tones in graphite. These effects may be related to the different lighting effects, highlights in images, and varying levels of darkness. To achieve success with shading in pyrography, it is a good idea to practice pencil shading techniques on paper and understand the transitions that happen as you move between light and dark areas.

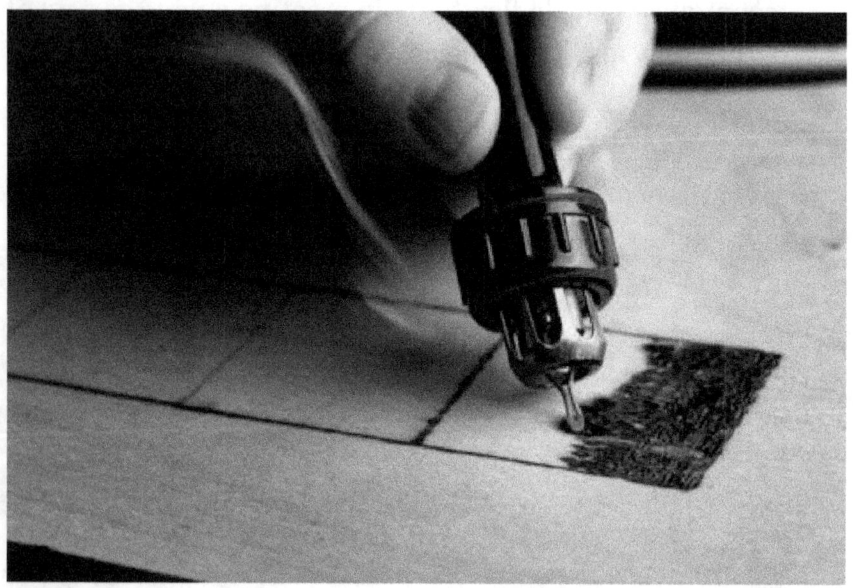

Things to Remember in Pyrography Shading

Chapter five on "Basic Line Techniques for Wood Burning" covers the core aspects of burning different types of lines in wood. You may also go back and refer to basic shading techniques discussed towards the end of the chapter. This chapter provides more information on shading and line art to achieve stunning pyrography artwork.

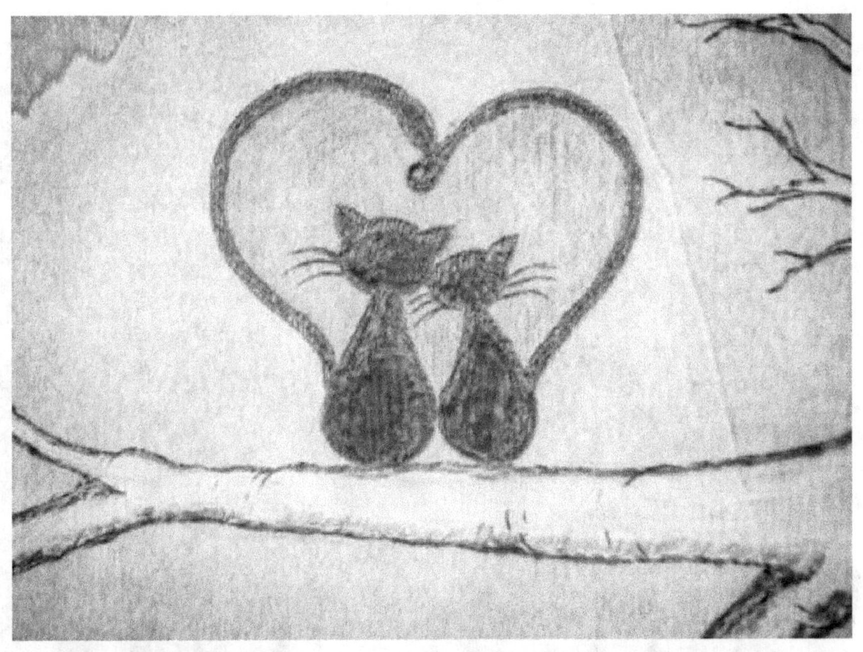

All types of shading in pyrography require the application of certain best practices, summarized below:

- Always start your artwork by drawing the outline of the desired image or transferring the image on wood.

- Start the burn process with a low temperature setting, and increase the temperature gradually.

- Apply only light pressure when burning the wood.

- Do not press your burn tool anytime while burning your pyrography artwork as it may lead to harsh lines, and you may not be able to either soften or erase them.

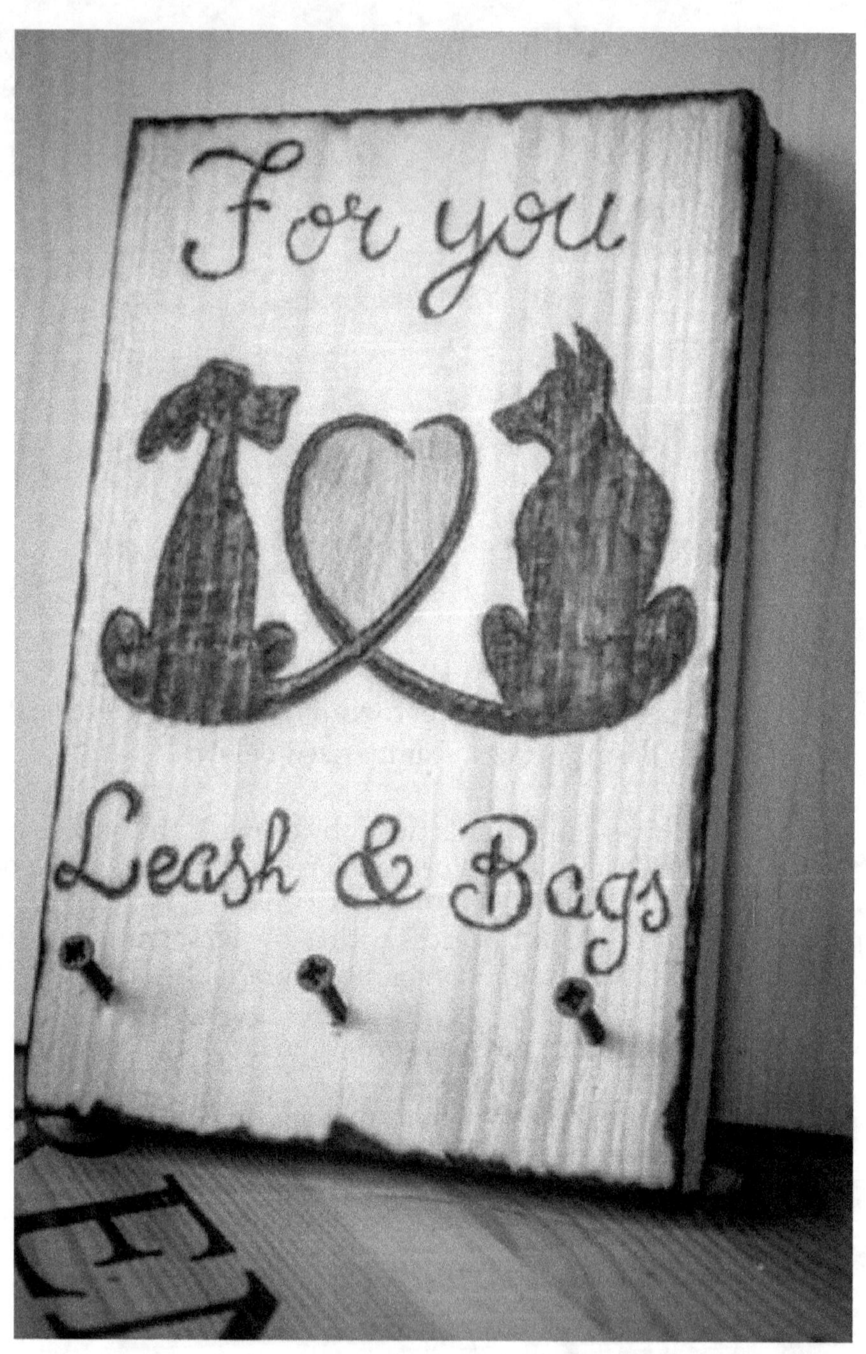

- Vary your shading intensity so that the dark and light regions are conspicuous and blend well together.

- When moving between light and dark areas, make slow movements with your pen. Increase temperature when you want to color dark areas and decrease the intensity of heat in order to achieve lighter tones.

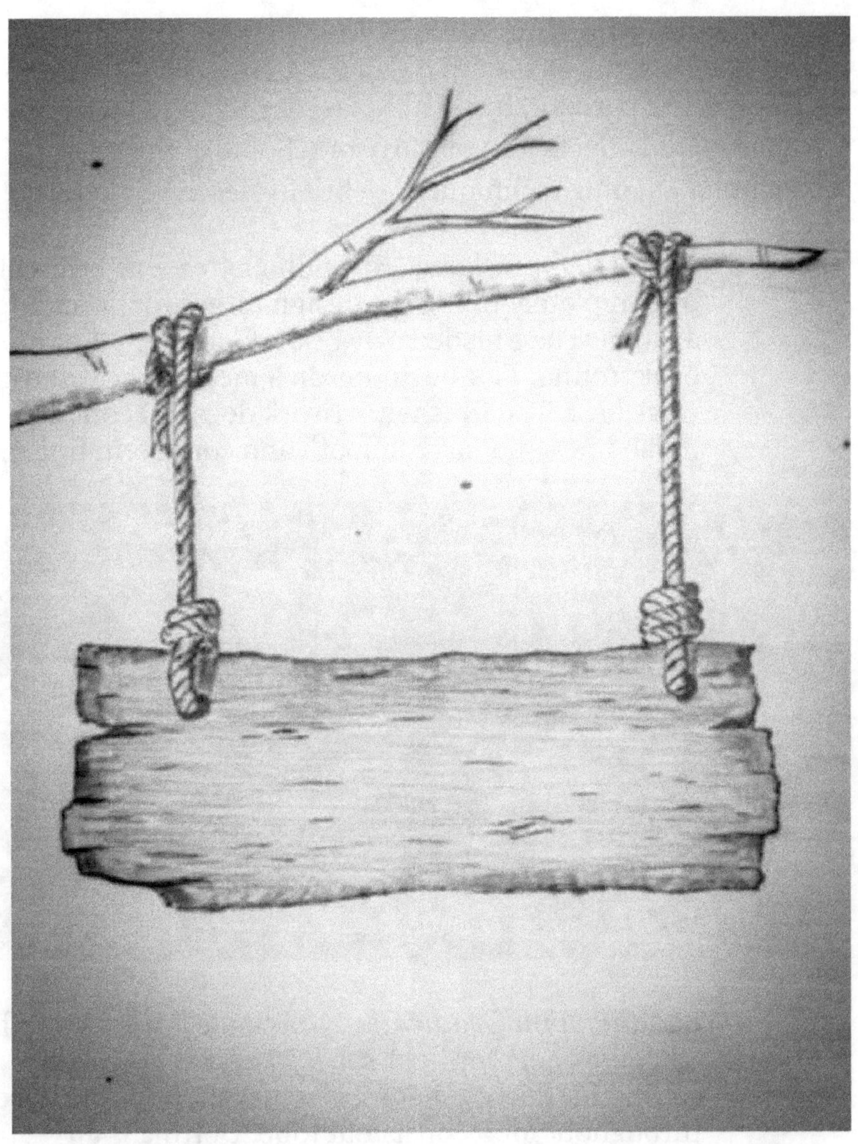

- An effective approach in shading is to start on low temperature, burning small and tight circles on wood.

Continue the circular motion until a light and consistent shade is achieved. The best shading is achieved when you cannot make out where it started and where it ended in your finished piece of art.

Common Shading Techniques

Several pyrography techniques may be used to achieve the desired effects for your artwork. Some of the most popular shading techniques are briefly described below:

- *Solid Fill for Silhouettes* – Silhouettes may be created by completely filling the design rather than shading an area. The finished artwork is black with the wood background. Flat burn tips on a medium heat setting work best. The finished artwork does not contain harsh lines and has a smooth and consistent finish.

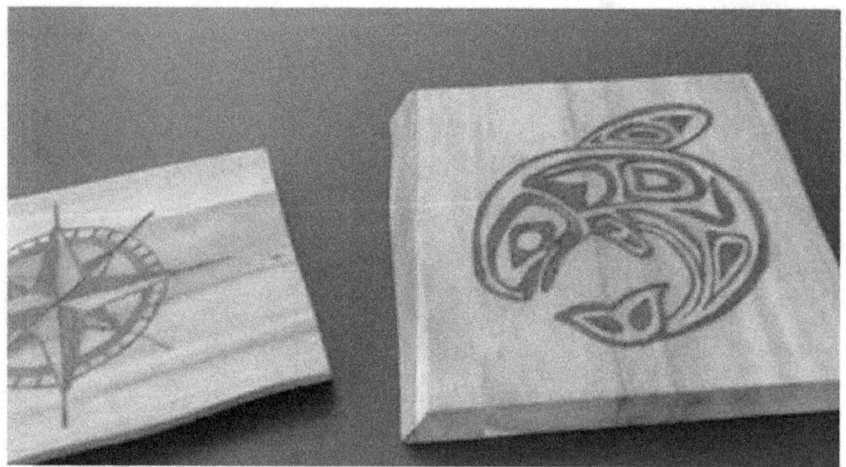

- *Shading with Gradients* – Gradients are achieved by using low heat for light shades and a higher heat setting for darker shades. Circular motions are used throughout for a consistent tone. Dotting is an important method to achieve consistent shades on wood. Using this technique, small dots are created on wood to achieve an even tone. To get darker tones, the dotting is done on a higher temperature setting.

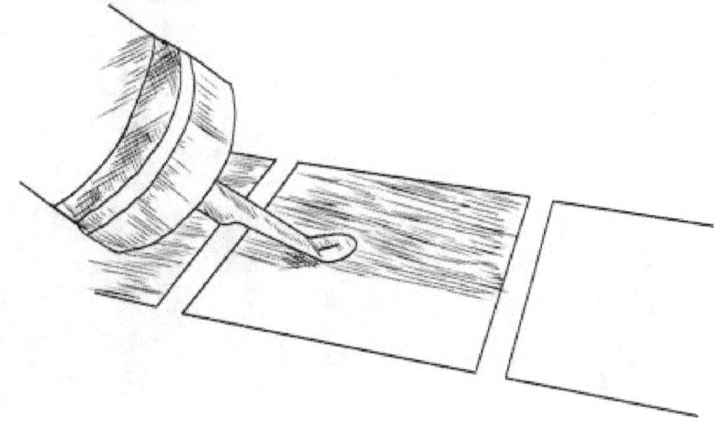

- *Hatching* – In hatching, thin lines are burnt in a single direction, followed by cross hatches in the opposite direction. Cross-hatching creates a darker overall tone. Hatching may sometimes be preferred over shading to achieve a consistent tone over dark areas. Hatching and cross-hatching may also be useful when creating a wide variety of designs.

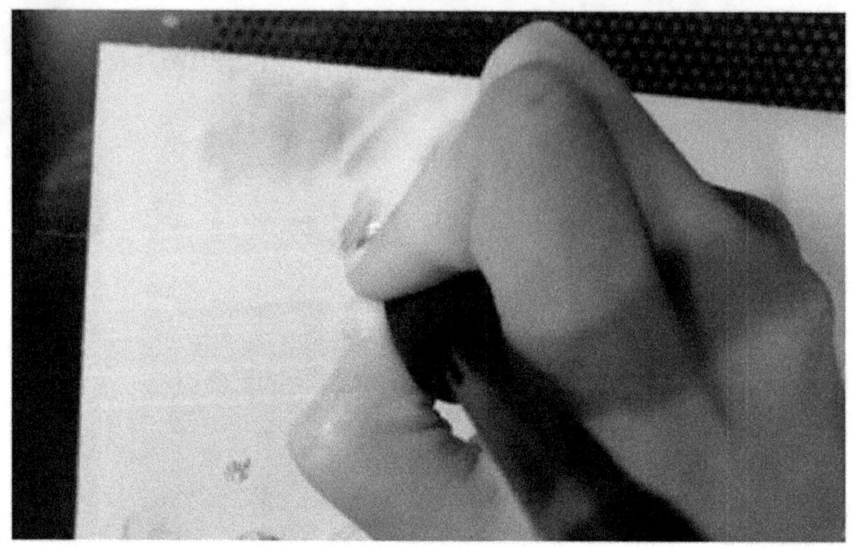

- *Creating Textures* – Textures may be created using the flat tip or skew tip. Several textures such as hair, feathers, and fur may be created for realistic artworks with a three-dimensional aspect. In general, low heat and fast strokes achieve light textures while a higher heat setting and greater intensity of pressure produces darker textures.

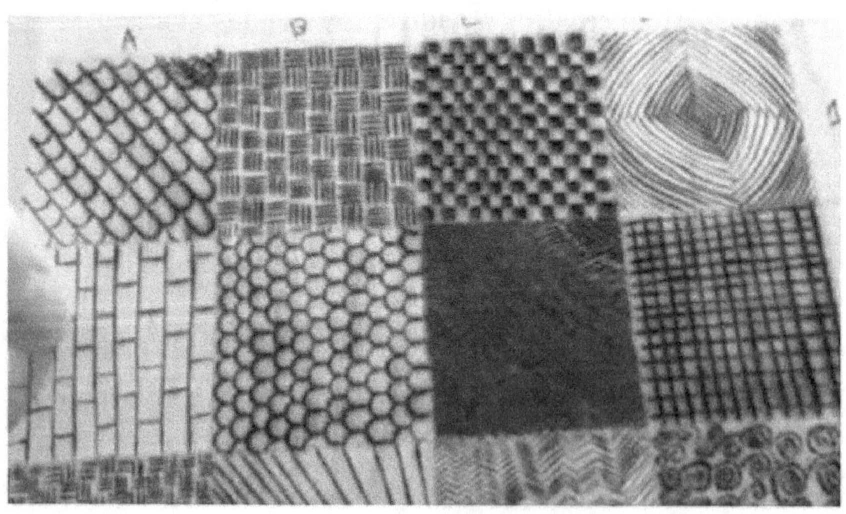

- *Burning Large Backgrounds* – Sometimes pyrography projects may require consistent backgrounds with a smooth and even finish. To effectively fill a background, use a wide pen tip to cover large areas with an even hue. A round pen tip works best and reduces the possibility of sharp strokes. Alternatively, pyrographers may settle for a torch for an even shading effect. Different effects may be achieved by varying shading styles in your background. For example, you could add focus to your image by retaining a light background around the image and creating a darker shade around the border. To get a dark, near-black background for your pyrography artwork, pull the pen tip across the background area using slow and consistent strokes.

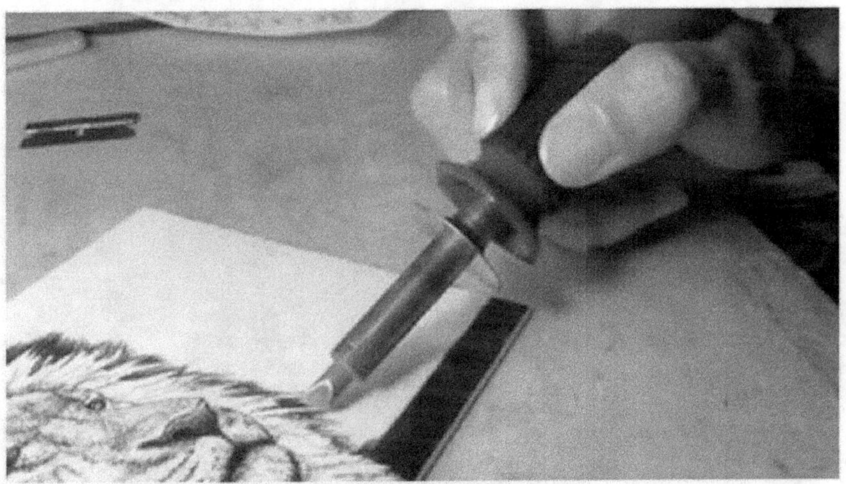

Pyrography Shading Exercise

Shading by burning on wood requires patience and practice. Follow the simple exercises mentioned below to achieve expertise in shading on wood.

- Draw a rectangle across the length of your wooden block and divide it into squares with approximately equal dimensions

- Start by filling the first square with light pressure on medium heat. Use the edge of your pen and incorporate short strokes in a single direction until you fill the entire area.

- Now move onto the next square and start filling the area. This time, apply a little more pressure on the same medium setting to achieve a darker shade.

- Continue moving forward, one square at a time, increasing the intensity of pressure as you go. The final result must be visible in the form of a row of squares in increasing level of burn intensity, producing darker shades every time.

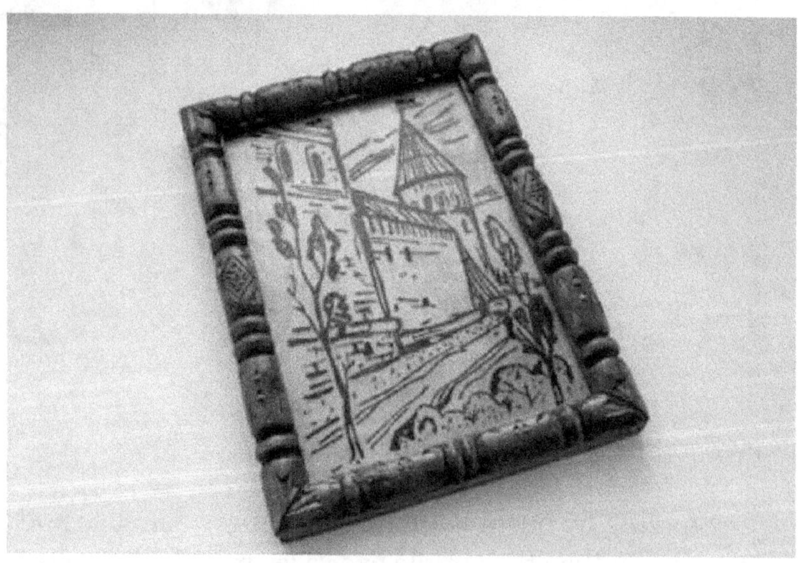

Chapter Summary

- Shading adds depth to your artwork, and helps achieve different tones of darkness.

- Shading techniques for pencil sketching may be directly applied to achieve the desired shading in your pyrography artwork.

- Follow best practices when applying shading techniques to your pyrography projects:

  o Transfer the image outline to wood prior to burning it.

  o Use light pressure as pressing the burn tool may produce conspicuous strokes.

  o Start with a low temperature setting, increasing gradually as you go.

  o Vary shading intensity to blend light and dark regions well.

  o Increasing the intensity of heat produces darker tones.

  o Use circular motion for even shading.

- Some of the common shading techniques useful for most pyrography projects are solid fill silhouettes (filling the design with a dark tone), shading using gradients, hatching in one direction followed by cross-hatches in the opposite direction, and creating textures and backgrounds.

- A simple shading exercise in pyrography will help you understand how shading works. In this exercise, you draw a rectangle and then divide it into equal squares. Then you start shading the squares, starting with lighter tones and then progressing towards a darker tone. The purpose is to precisely understand and compare the different heat settings and identify the nature of shading they produce.

In the next chapter you will learn how to burn common landscape elements.

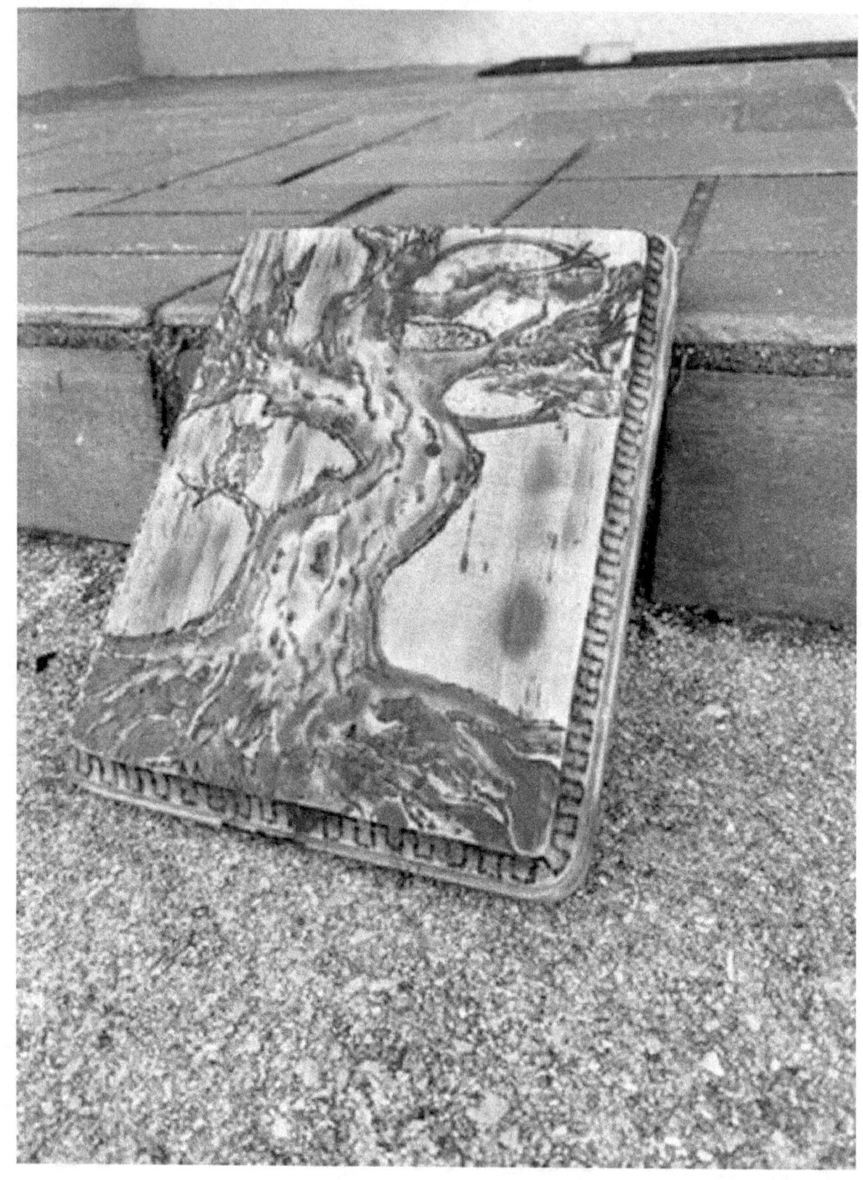

Chapter Thirteen:
Wood Burning Common Landscape

Burning landscapes on wood can produce beautiful pieces of art. Pyrographers use a variety of textures and dramatic tones to achieve landscapes depicting life-like scenes. Landscapes are a rich form of pyrography artwork as the artist gets the opportunity to try different patterns and effects to portray the different features of landscapes.

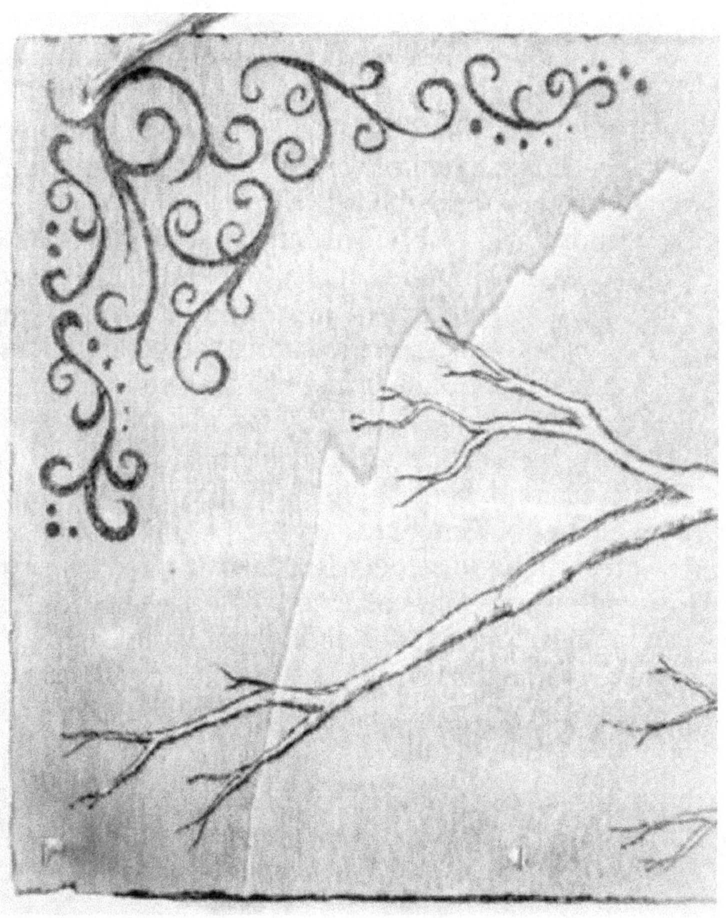

A basic walkthrough of creating a simple landscape is described in a step-by-step process below.

- Draw your desired landscape on paper or print a digital image of your chosen landscape.

- Transfer the landscape you intend to burn on your piece of wood. You may use any of the transfer techniques such as placing a carbon paper on wood and then placing the image over it to trace and obtain an impression on wood. More information on transfer techniques is covered on Chapter seven on "Image Transfer Techniques".

- Burn the outline of your landscape with the tip of your pen tool. Fill the required areas with patterns and gradients. Shading is covered briefly in Chapter five on "Basic Line Techniques for Wood Burning". Further, Chapter Twelve provides detailed information on line art and shading and discusses the several techniques of shading and backgrounds that you may incorporate in your landscape. In line with the techniques covered here, you could define dark areas of your landscape by using solid fill for silhouettes or shading light and dark gradients by varying heat. You could use this technique to define areas representing the land, sky, sea, or other elements. Hatching serves as a good wood burning technique to achieve the desired effects for trees and mountains and you could experiment with textures to achieve the right level of detail for specific elements in your imaginative landscape art. Finally, you could highlight your image using a suitable background definition technique.

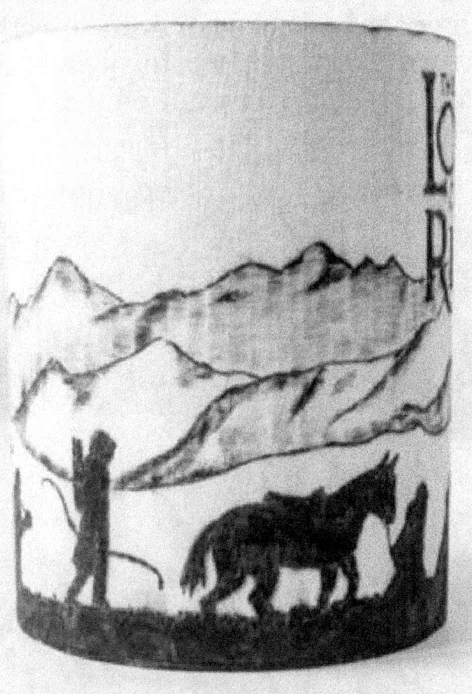

Recommended Wood Burning Techniques for Landscape Elements

Although wood burning landscapes is a flexible technique, and you could use a technique of your choice to achieve the intended effect, certain tried and tested methods, described below, produce life-like artwork.

- *Wood Burning Mountains* - Burn the outline to start with, and then use the hatching technique to accentuate the top and sides of the mountain to achieve a three-dimensional effect. Shading may also be used to achieve life-like artwork of rocks and mountains. When shading rocks and mountains, you may work with the direction of light to shade areas depicting shadows in a darker tone, while leaving the original wood color for areas directly facing the light source. You may select the light and dark areas in your art much like you would in any pencil shading project.

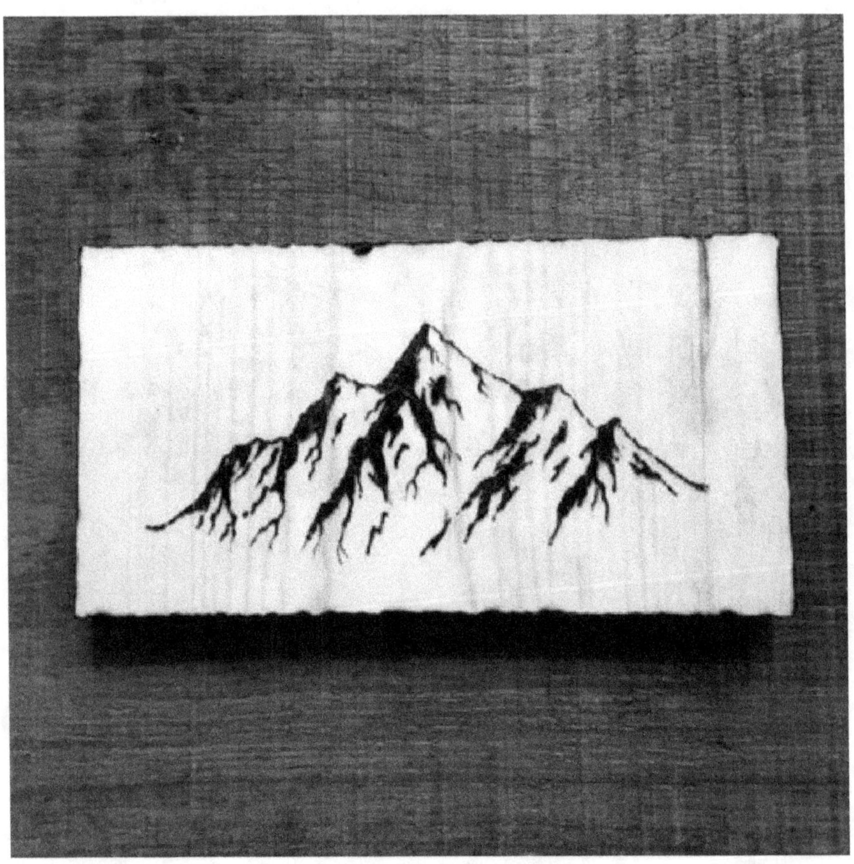

- *Burning Tree Barks* – Burning a tree bark requires considerable skill and imagination. A tree bark consists of several light and dark regions. The hollow areas of a tree bark are dark, while the areas surrounding them are lighter with a high level of detail. To start burning a region of the tree bark, burn a blob in a small area to define the darkest region. Mark outlines for the blob using your pen tip.

Defining the outlines essentially frames the blob defined earlier. The areas between the blob and outline remain the lightest to produce the desired effect. Next, you may shade the area surrounding the blob and outline in a way that defines contours of the tree bark. You may use dotting to define a realistic background. The last step is to burn thin lines in the direction of contours of the tree bark. This texture may be defined for several regions to achieve your final artwork.

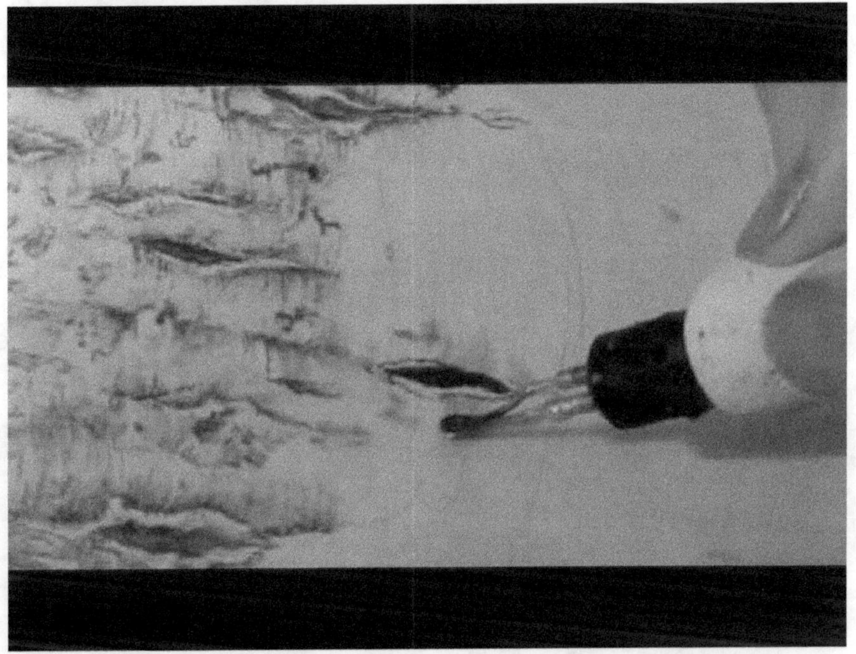

- *Wood Burning Waves* – To wood burn waves, burn the outline first. Then draw equally spaced curves along the wave. Finally, add strokes in a single direction to depict the wave. Use shading to fill areas between two curves. Accentuate the wave by applying repeated strokes at the top of the wave, while retaining a lighter tone for the rest of the wave. Repeat the steps for more waves to achieve overlapping ocean waves.

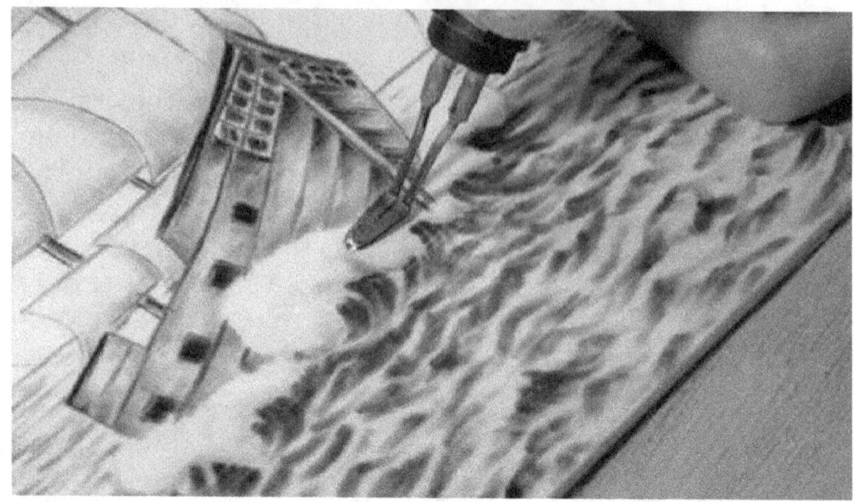

- *Wood Burning Clouds* – Wood burning clouds require intricate shading to represent their light and dark regions. Although the shading intensity of clouds is generally light, regions on the periphery of the cloud are shaded in a darker tone, while those near the center are left in the original color of the wood. The shape of the cloud is also defined using light tones.

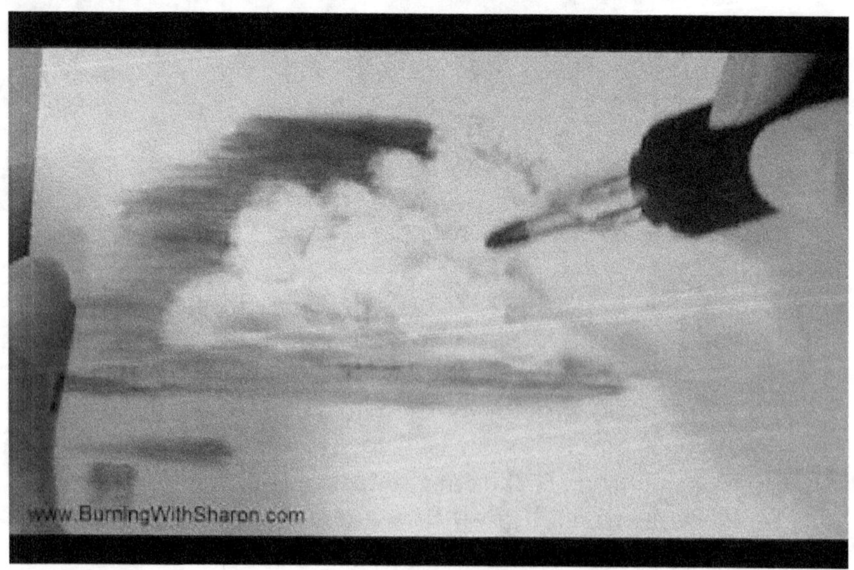

The techniques covered in this chapter provide good starting points to wood burn other elements of landscapes. These techniques may be varied or extended to achieve an unlimited number of methods to define realistic landscape elements. Finally, experience is the best teacher, and your unique understanding of burn tools, tips, and the effects achieved on wood will eventually help you define real landscapes in wood.

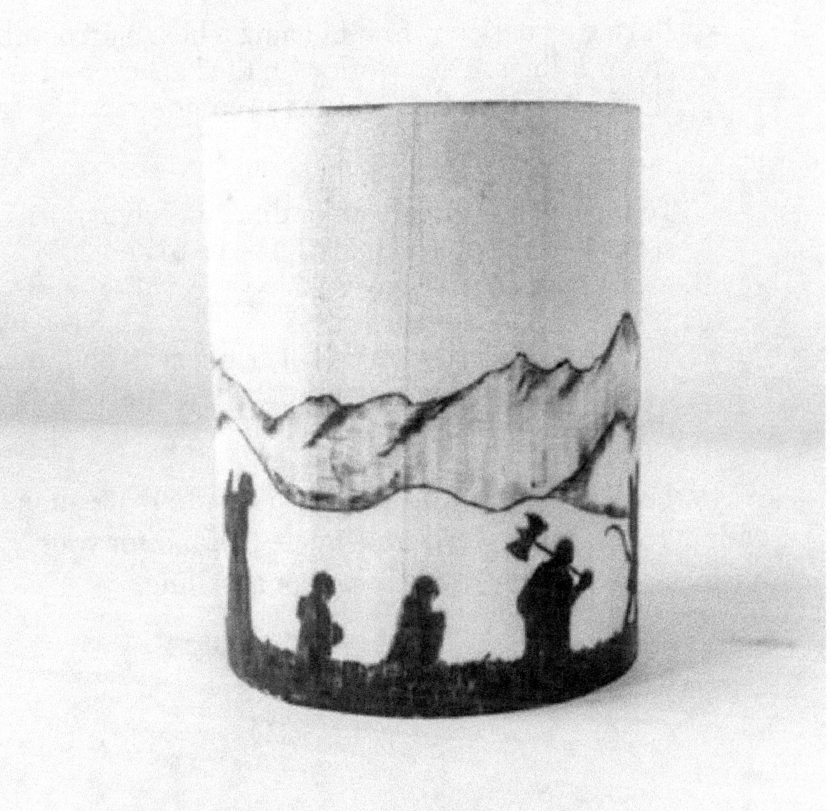

Chapter Summary

- Similar to most pyrography artwork, you may start burning landscape elements by transferring the design on wood by either drawing it or obtaining an impression using a transfer technique.

- Start by burning the landscape outline and then burn textures, shades, and gradients for its different elements.

- To burn mountains, use hatching or shading to darken the top and sides of mountains while leaving certain other areas exposed to light.

- Burn tree barks by first burning a blob, surrounded by contour lines. Then work with the background and shade and draw lines along the contours on the tree bark.

- To burn waves, create an outline, and then burn strokes in the direction of the wave to depict overlapping ocean waves.

- To burn clouds, shade their periphery to obtain a darker shade while retaining the light parts around the center of the cloud.

In the next chapter you will learn how to make money with pyrography artwork, and create a brand for your business, as well as engage in personal selling.

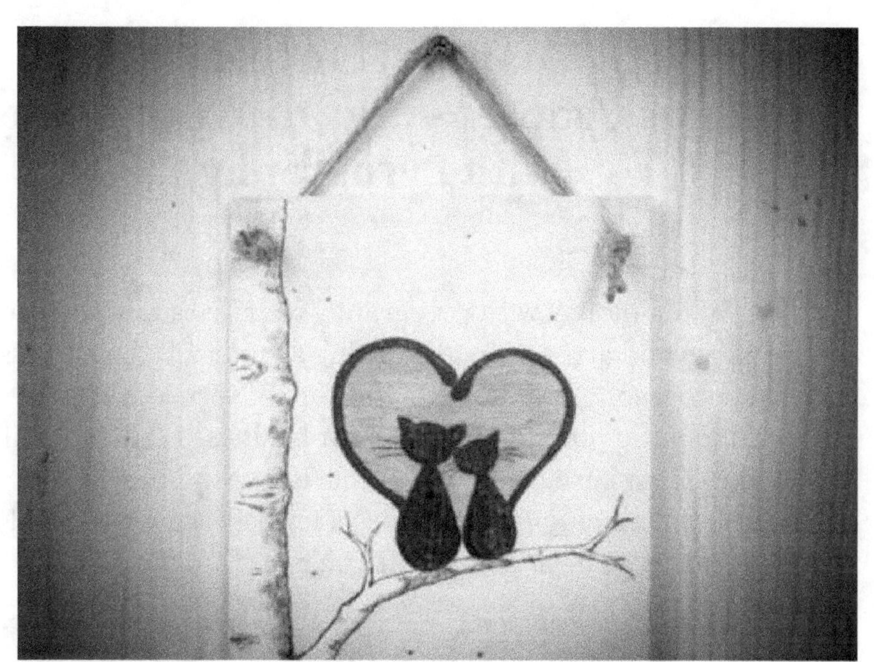

Chapter Fourteen: Bonus Chapter - How to Make Money with Pyrography

Making money with pyrography requires a few additional skills beyond artistic wood-burning acumen. To be successful in a pyrography business, you need to advertise your artwork in art galleries and fairs. Once your business is able to build a decent client base, you may be able to expand into international markets. There are a few key areas you need to focus on, to achieve a successful business.

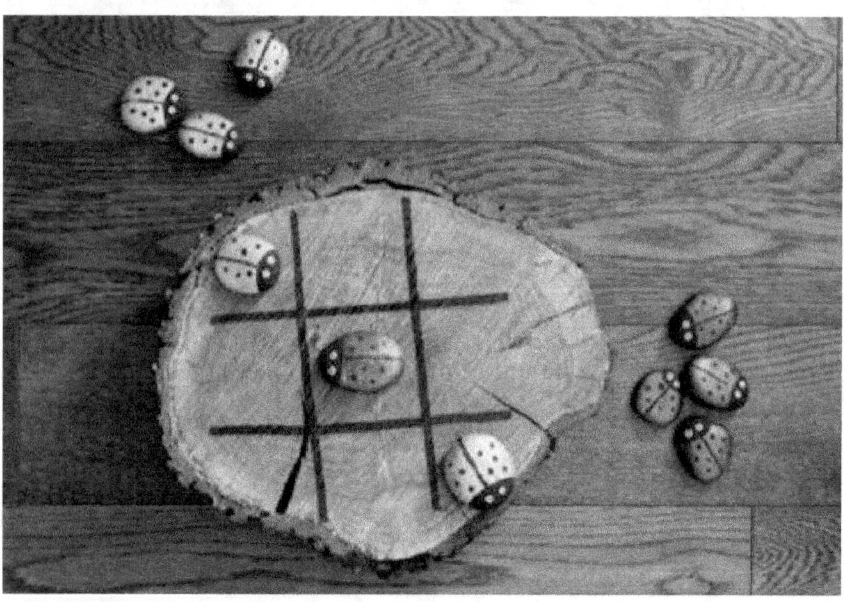

Selling Your Artwork – When you start out as a new business owner, it is possible to get people interested in your artwork. You can simply educate visitors and enlighten them on the creativity involved. This strategy helps to motivate them to invest in your artwork. You could even demonstrate

a wood-burning session to make them familiar with the
equipment used in this unique form of artwork.

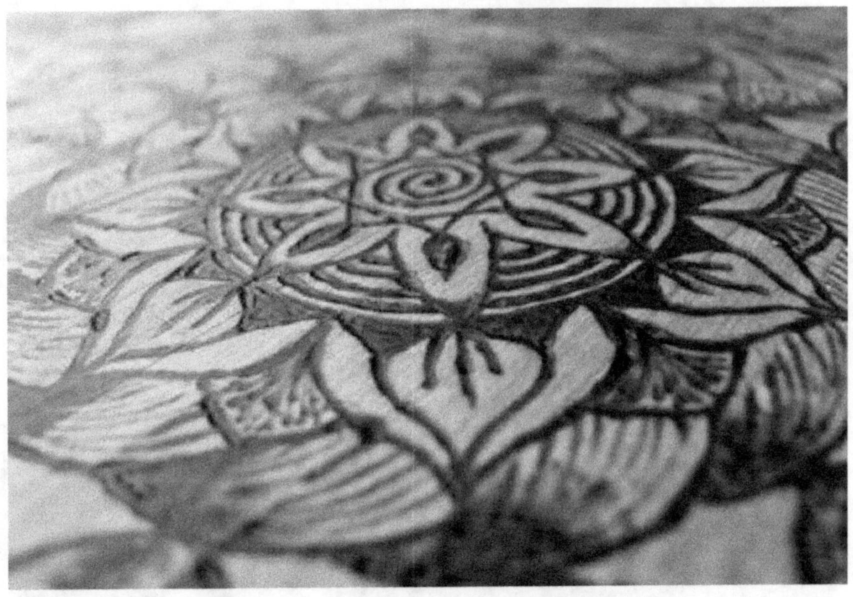

Conducting Pyrography Classes – Besides selling
finished pyrography artwork, you could also function as a
pyrography instructor, delivering workshops according to a
convenient schedule. You could organize workshops at local
art organizations or you may conduct one-to-one sessions.
There are several opportunities to enrich your workshops by
including hands-on pyrography projects. Workshops serve as
a good means of income as they provide the flexibility of
charging fees as per your discretion. It is a good idea to set
up a fee structure based on the cost of tools, materials used,
electricity, and other items.

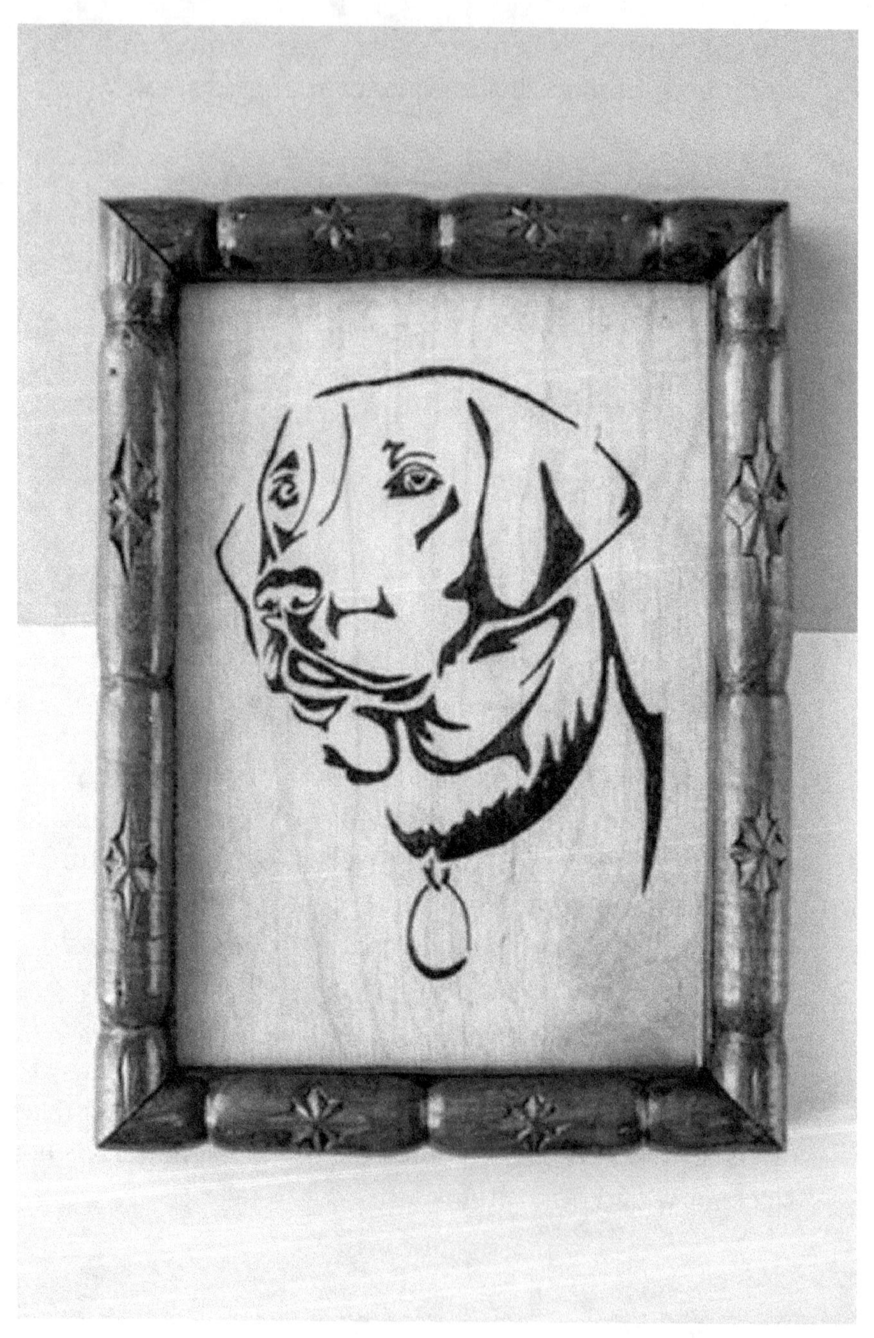

Advertising Online and Offline – Whether you are selling your artwork or offering classes focusing on pyrography, advertising and promotions is a key aspect of your successful business. The different forms of advertising include word-of-mouth promotions, demonstrations, and internet-based networking and promotions. Several popular online platforms such as Fiverr and Freelancer.com offer simple tools and methods to enlist and display artwork. The online platforms have an elaborate marketing and promotions strategy to systematically connect buyers and sellers for a continuous income stream. Most crafters and artists find it lucrative to sell using the available online platforms.

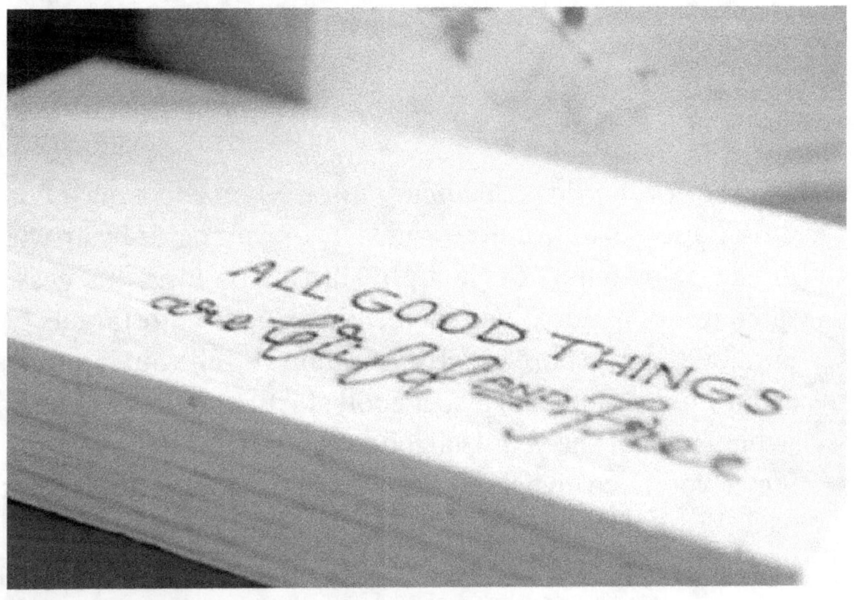

Retail Options for Selling your Pyrography Art – The place to sell your finished artwork is at a local outlet. Local craft shows are also accessible places to display your artwork. Another option is to display it at a retail outlet that accepts products from independent artists and displays them to prospective customers.

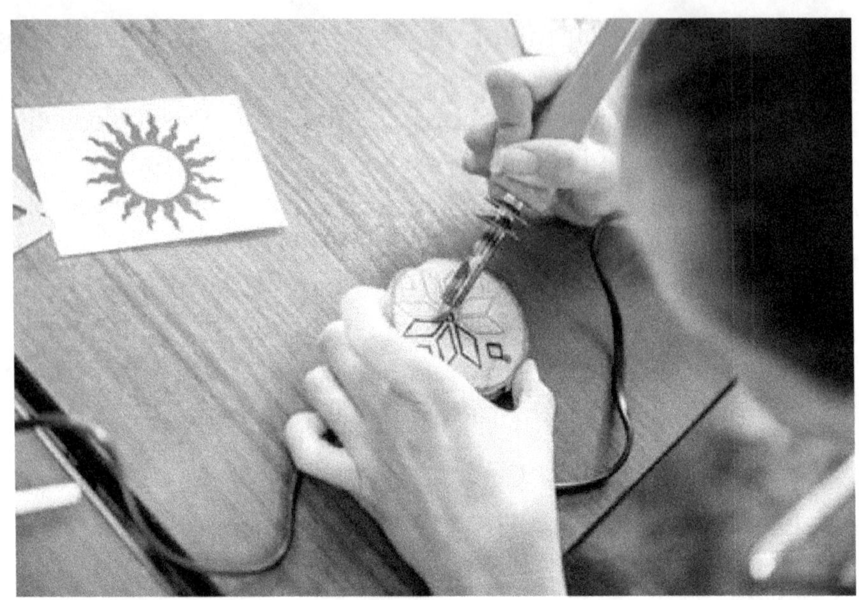

Working with a Business Plan - When choosing among retail options to promote and sell your pyrography artwork, a business plan may be the right starting point. A business plan is a strategic way to determine who is your target audience and where exactly you want to sell your products. Your business plan is also a good starting point to determine which part of the year is a good time to sell your artwork. Once you have answered these basic questions, it is time to sell through the channels predetermined for the purpose. You may use a variety of marketing tools such as cold calling, setting up a website, email marketing, creating multiple landing pages, and promoting through social media pages (Facebook, Twitter, LinkedIn, and the like).

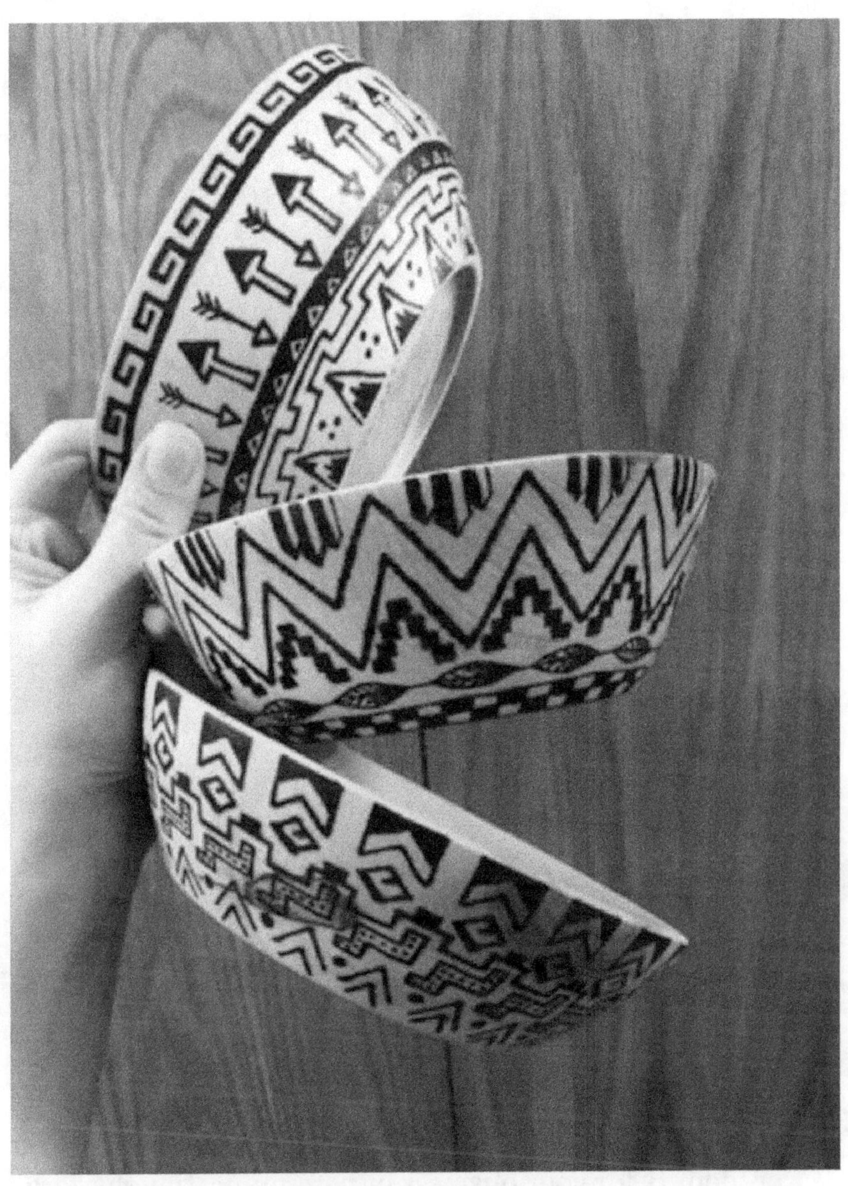

Create your Brand and Invest in Personal Selling

Brand marketing and personal selling are two important concepts every business owner must learn. A brand is an identity that a business owner builds for his/her personal undertaking. The business owner must answer several questions to successfully create a unique brand. These questions include aspects related to the look and feel of the business, and the perception of your business by your target audience.

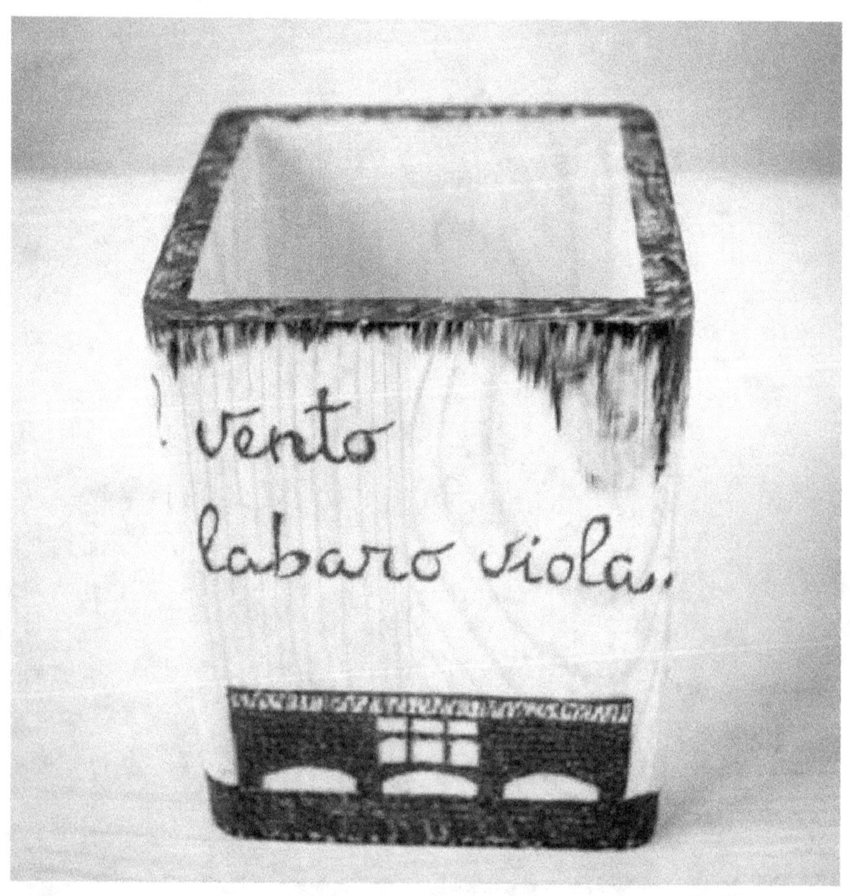

Branding - As a business owner, you can create a brand or identity for your business by communicating the core focus of your business with a logo and tagline. The logo and tagline sets you apart from competition in your market space. You can create a lasting impression in the minds of your target audience by promoting it with an impressive name. Your logo must be designed to convincingly relate your unique style and product. A slogan or tagline usually accompanies your logo and communicates the core focus of your business in the form of a message. Thereafter, the strategy of any business owner is to apply the brand across offline and online platforms.

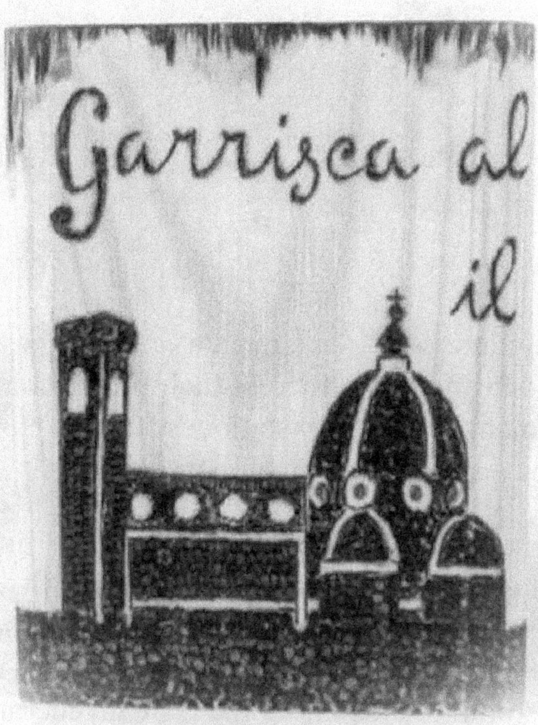

Communicating your message effectively requires you to identify your customers and competitors. Creative business owners often employ diverse strategies in branding such as using metaphors, colors that relate to different emotions, and suitable fonts. Once you have identified a brand and strategies to communicate your message, you must make sure it remains consistent across customer interactions.

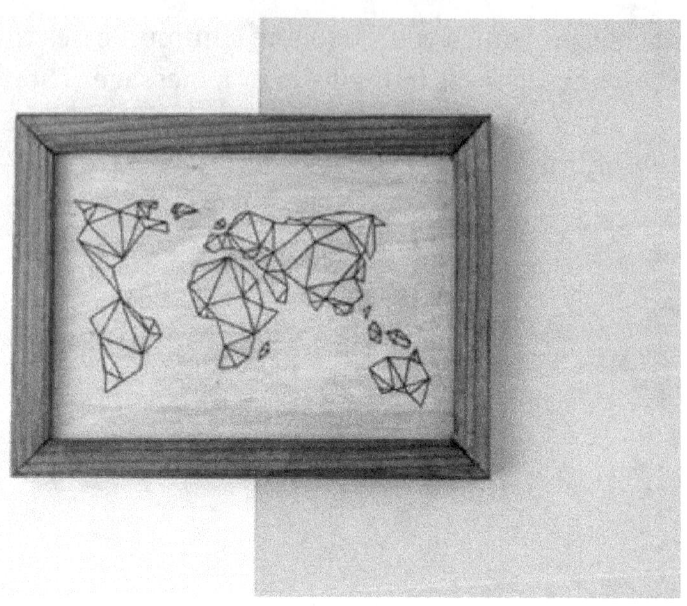

Business owners must make sure they have exactly the same logo and tagline across their promotional material, shipping materials, and stationery to help customers recognize and connect with their business.

Personal Selling - Further to branding, another important aspect that would benefit your pyrography business is personal selling. In the personal selling approach, businesses sell products in their face-to-face meeting with the customer. Personal selling is highly lucrative for pyrography professionals as business owners get the opportunity to effectively promote their product or service and are able to influence their selling by leveraging their knowledge on the subject. In your personal selling encounter, you can demonstrate the art to your prospective customer and influence their buying decision by describing the creativity involved in the art.

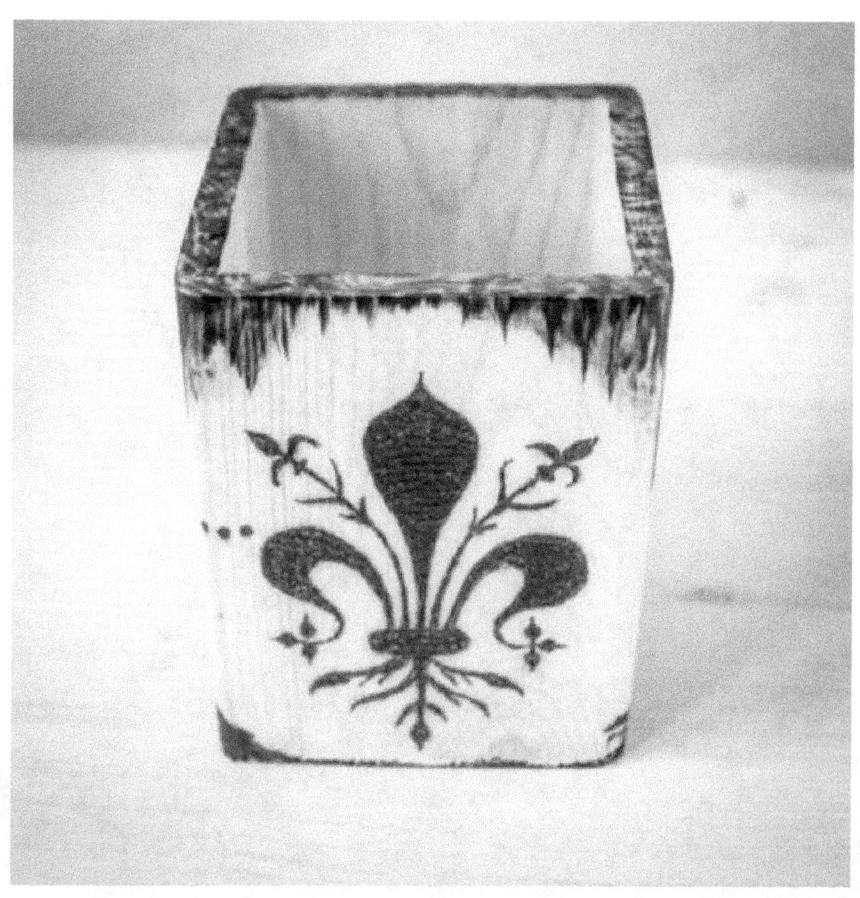

Personal selling offers a high level of attention to the customer and allows your message to be customized. The personal selling approach is an interactive strategy you can use to persuade your customers and adapt to their preferences. This allows you to customize your product to cater to their tastes and preferences.

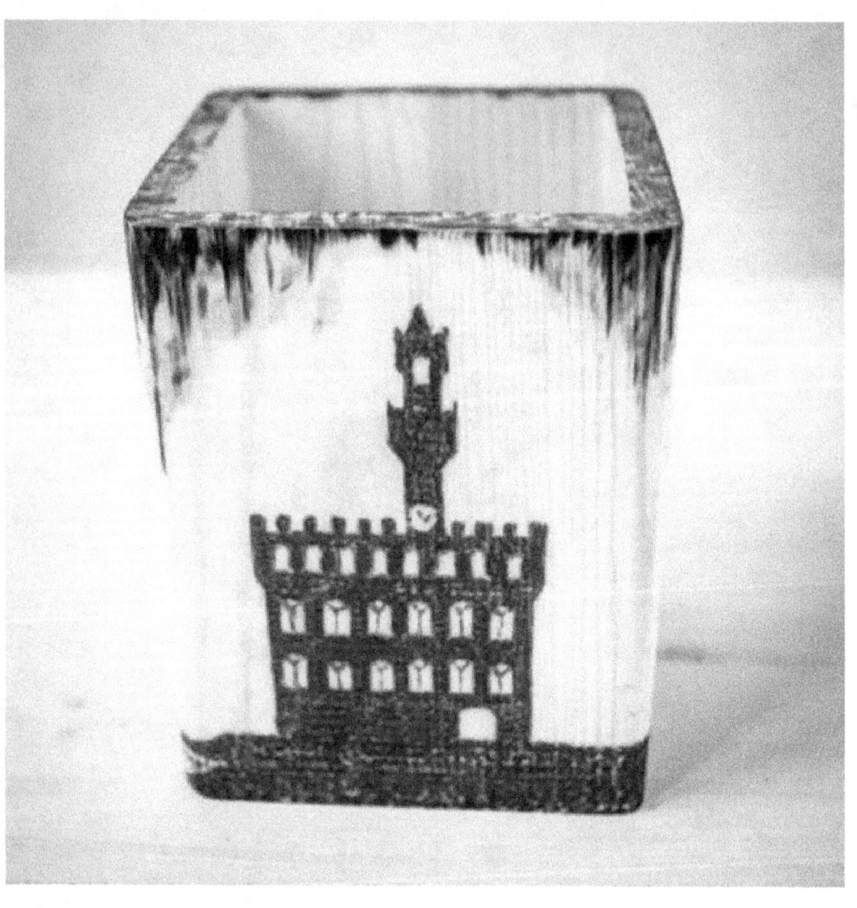

Chapter Summary

- Making money with pyrography is a lucrative initiative and has potential of success.

- Business owners dealing in pyrography artwork are expected to undertake the marketing and promotions of their online business.

- Building a good client base leads to their participation in international markets.

- Pyrography artists may undertake various strategies to set up a successful business.

- o Any business needs clients and it is important to get people interested in your product offering. Create interest in your existing visitors by educating them on the technique and helping them understand the creative process. Motivate your visitors through demonstrations of your unique art.

  - o Another important source of income is by conducting regular pyrography classes and workshops. Consult local organizations that encourage artwork and conduct one-to-one sessions. Organize hands-on activities to attract prospective students and charge appropriately.

  - o Advertising is an important aspect of getting your word around. To sustain a successful business, conduct different forms of advertising including demonstrations, word-of-mouth advertising, and advertising via internet and online media. Reach out to your target market through established platforms such as Freelancer-com and Fiverr.

  - o Approaching local retail marketplaces to display your artwork to their customer base is an effective strategy to get your product out into the local market

- Business owners must oversee the following aspects besides producing professional pyrography artwork.

  - o Create a business plan with objectives related to growing your business and promoting your pyrography artwork.

  - o Determine the right time to complete your selling process and operate through a wide variety of marketing tools. Use cold calling, email marketing, product promotion through a website and social media platforms to increase your sales.

- o Keep track of your customers and competitors

- Branding is another important aspect of your successful business.

  - o Create a brand identity and communicate its core focus.

  - o Work with a logo and tagline to communicate your core message.

  - o Think of an impressive name for your business to attract clients.

  - o Maintain a consistent look and feel for your logo to depict your unique product and style of undertaking your business.

  - o Use diverse branding strategies such as unique fonts, metaphors, and colors representing emotions to communicate the purpose of your business.

  - o Use your brand across online and offline platforms to help customers identify with your business.

- Personal selling is another area pyrography artists may explore to increase sales.

  - o Personal selling is a way to effectively promote your product and sell it to customers in a face-to-face meeting.

  - o In personal selling, you use your knowledge of the subject to influence your prospective clients and guide them to a "buy" decision.

  - o The technique is effective as it involves a high level of attention for your customer.

o   You get to customize your brand message and influence prospective customers.

o   You also get the opportunity to customize your product according to the tastes and preferences of your customers.

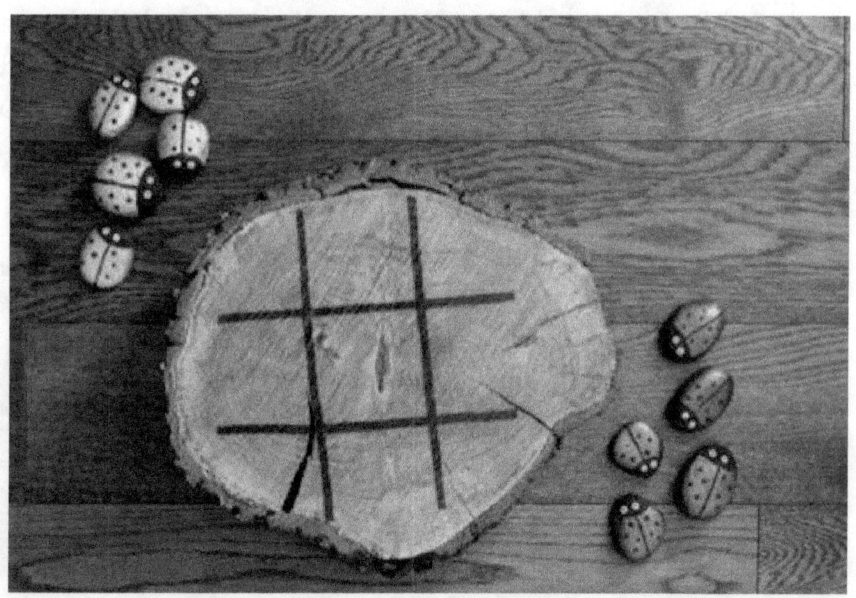

Final Words

Wood burning or pyrography is a highly rewarding skill and is practiced worldwide. It is a creative pursuit and requires the knowledge of line art, shading, and shadows to create a wide variety of designs on wood. Pyrography traces its origin to Greece and has been in wide use since the 1900s. It has been an integral part of cultures in China, Egypt, Rome, and Peru.

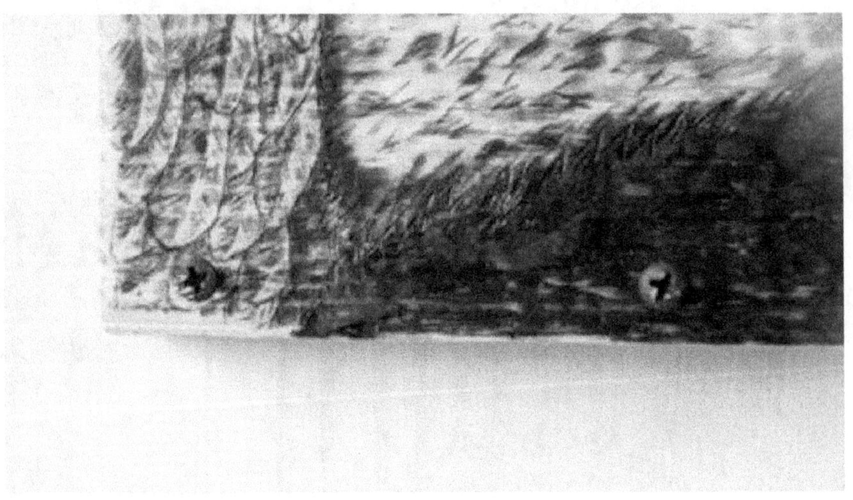

Pyrograpgers need an in-depth understanding of wood surfaces and as well as how they react to heat to obtain different types of textures. Maple, baswood, beech, poplar, red oak, birch, and pine may be used for pyrography projects. Each type of wood has its own pros and cons. Selecting the right wood burning tool from among wire-nib burners, solid point wood burners, and laser wood burning pens may be accomplished based on the type of effect you would like to achieve on the surface of wood. Burn tools have different types of burn tips to burn lines, fill shaded portions, and draw calligraphy lines.Your choice of the right burn tip influences the overall quality of your artwork. Furthermore, holding and working effectively with the burn tool is an essential skill you must acquire. Safety is an important consideration, and pyrographers must take care of ventilation, the use of face masks, and exhaust fans, as well as handling hot burn tools.

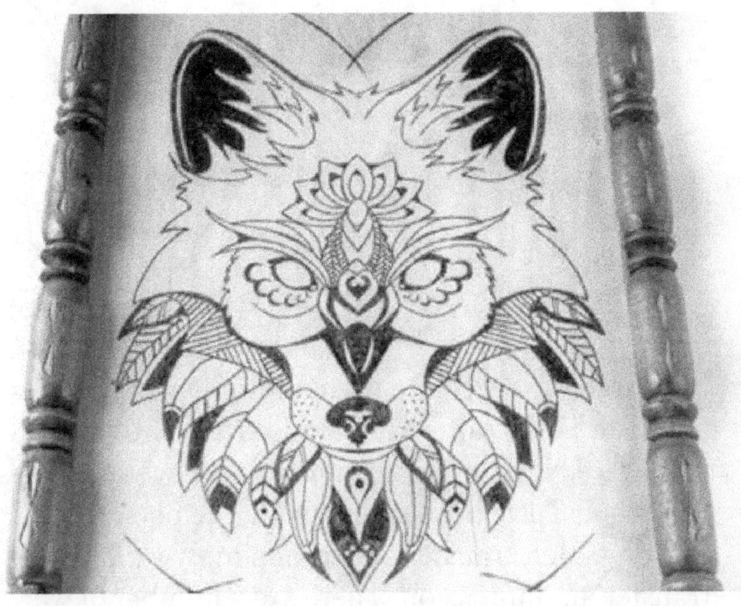

Learning to produce your own USB-powered burn tool, as explained in the book, also helps you understand how burners and burn tips work. The next step is to learn line art encompassing precise steps to draw lines, curves, waves, dots, and meandering lines, as well as techniques for shading, textures, and gradients.

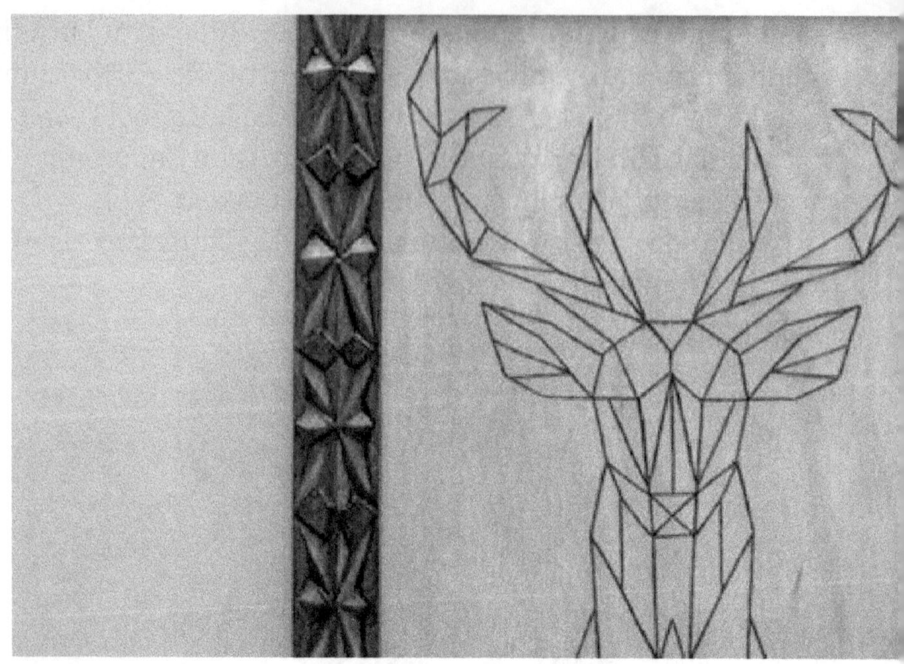

To effectively create pyrography artwork, it is essential to understand the different ways to transfer digital images with the desired level of detail onto wood. Several images transfer techniques have been discussed in the book such as using carbon paper, transfer paper, or simply rubbing the image to transfer an impression. There are a number of ways to produce beautiful pyrography artwork such as using stencils to burn designs on wood. Another technique is to burn Lichtenberg figures using a high voltage discharge. The technique must be learned with in-depth safety precautions to be able to produce professional artwork. Another creative technique to produce professional art is burning the mandala using a stencil and covering the artwork with epoxy. Important considerations on using epoxy effectively to finish your project are covered in the book and may be applied to most of your finished artwork.

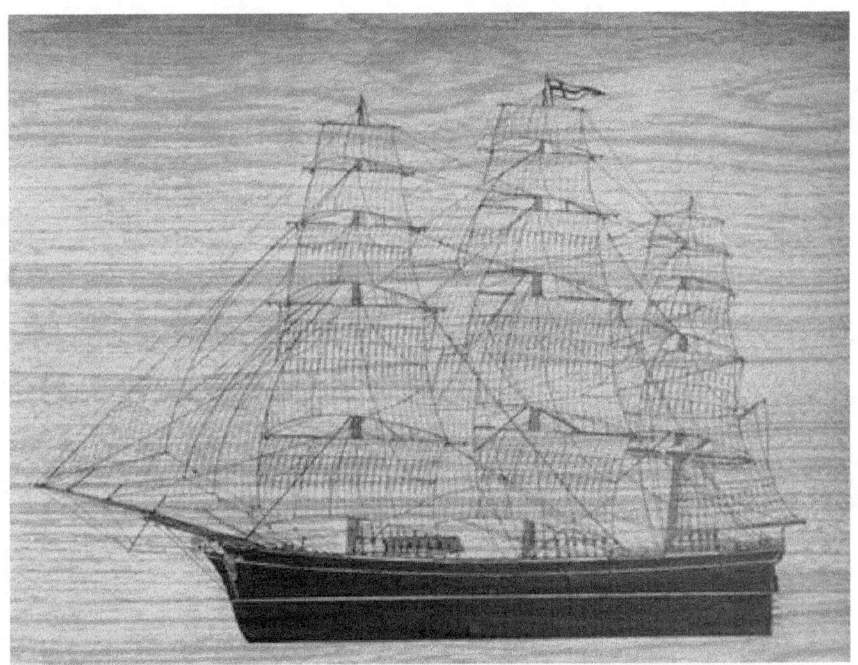

Step-by-step instructions to burn a Christmas Box and create fridge magnets are also covered in the book. As you progress, it is important to understand how to implement advanced shading and gradient techniques and apply them to burning landscape elements on wood. Learning to burn the right kind of effects and textures that resemble water, mountains, tree barks, and clouds helps you achieve a number of creative effects and textures in professional pyrography projects. Towards the end, the book wraps the leisure pursuit to enlighten prospective business owners with the tools and skills they require to establish a thriving business.

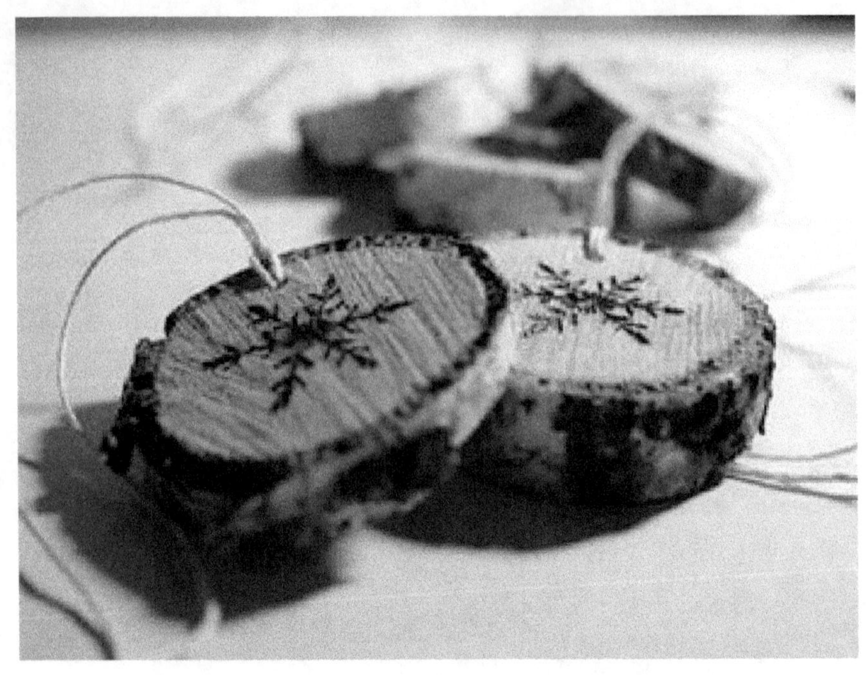

Image Credit: www.Shutterstock.com